Living on the Horns of Dilemmas

Other Books By the Authors

The Dark Side of Educational Leadership: Superintendents and the Professional Victim Syndrome

Living on the Horns of Dilemmas

Superintendents, Politics, and Decision-Making

Peter Litchka, Walter Polka,
and Frank Calzi

Published in partnership with
the American Association of School Administrators
ROWMAN & LITTLEFIELD
Lanham • Boulder • New York • London

Published in partnership with the American Association of School Administrators

Published by Rowman & Littlefield
A wholly owned subsidiary of The Rowman & Littlefield Publishing Group, Inc.
4501 Forbes Boulevard, Suite 200, Lanham, Maryland 20706
www.rowman.com

16 Carlisle Street, London W1D 3BT, United Kingdom

British Library Cataloguing in Publication Information Available

Library of Congress Cataloging-in-Publication Data Available

978-1-4758-0015-9 (cloth : alk. paper)
978-1-4758-0016-6 (pbk. : alk. paper)
978-1-4758-0017-3 (electronic)

♾ ™ The paper used in this publication meets the minimum requirements of American National Standard for Information Sciences Permanence of Paper for Printed Library Materials, ANSI/NISO Z39.48-1992.

Printed in the United States of America

To Reverend Dr. Stephen J. Denig, C.M.
(1948–2013)
Whose spirit and faith guided many of us to places we never have been!
Thank You, Father!

Contents

Acknowledgments

Pete:

For Don, Ed, and Greg: *Role models, colleagues, leaders, and friends!*

For Izzy, my wife of more than forty years: *It just keeps getting better all the time!*

For my son, Joe, my daughter, Annie, and her new husband, Danny.

Walt:

For my wife Vicky, daughters Jennifer and Monica, their husbands Jeff and Nate, and grandson Conner Walter and granddaughter Victoria Sharon: *Family Matters.*

Frank:

For Peter and Walt for their encouragement to help write this book.

For Vince Coppola and Norm Green who have practiced and know more about school leadership than any other educators I have known.

For my family who have provided many blessings in life—Marge, Steven, Beth Ann, David, Vanita, Jamie, John, Michael, Nicole, Rick, Jessica, Emily, Madelyn, and Jason.

From Pete, Frank, and Walt:

A special thanks to Rick Calzi for the artistic image on the cover of our book.

Thank you to Ms. Rosina Mete for her valuable research assistance and Dr. Rachael Ross for her valuable editing services.

For those superintendents who shared their stories:

We admire you, respect you, and thank you.

Foreword

As school superintendents we give more than our fair share of speeches. In 1999 I stood in front of my New York superintendent colleagues to accept the award for NYS Superintendent of the Year. I gave what was actually one of the best speeches of my career standing next to the NYS commissioner of education and gently criticized the state's fledgling emphasis on high stakes testing. At the time, I thought the overemphasis on testing would be a mistake. I now know I was right.

But the crux of that speech was not about testing; it was about the superintendency. I proceeded to lay out my argument as to why the position of superintendent of schools is the best job in any school district. It is the one position, I suggested, where you could impact the lives of every student in the district. You could set the tone, build the culture, drive the mission, you were the ultimate influencer, I argued—the one who could make the most significant difference.

Fifteen years later, after NCLB, RTT, the recession of 2008, after retiring as a twenty-three-year superintendent and spending eight years as a university professor, after running a dozen searches for superintendent positions, after developing a leadership coaching program that has touched over two hundred school leaders, after all that, I still think it's the best job in the district.

But it can be the worst.

Pete Litchka, Walt Polka, and Frank Calzi have been there. They have been in the ring with the bull(s) snorting around them. All three knew the code of the honor of the matador. All three lived the code, which for superintendents is straightforward. Do what is best for kids—always, do what is best for kids.

In any given year, the position of chief executive officer is listed as one of the ten most stressful jobs in America. I know a fair number of private sector CEOs and can attest that indeed they live a stressful life. Usually, however, a private sector CEO is given a powerful set of tools and broad decision-making authority to get the job done. In the private sector, the CEO is expected to bring in his or her own team. The board of directors may listen to shareholders, but won't be easily influenced by disgruntled employees or unsuccessful job seekers. The CEO is in command and is expected to develop strategies to drive profit margin, and develop new opportunities. The CEO who can grow the company and make money will be rewarded handsomely. According to the *Huffington Post*, average

CEO compensation stands at 354 times the compensation of the average worker. And that is not just for the superstars. JCPenney's CEO was making 1,795 times that of the average employee when he was asked to step away. And when it is time to leave, the private sector CEO inevitably, and seemingly regardless of performance, enjoys a generous severance package.

The CEO of a school district is in a very different situation. Upon taking office, he or she is greeted by the leadership team that is in place. If one of them was an unsuccessful candidate for the position, the superintendent just has to deal with that. The shareholders who elect the "board of directors" are the residents of the community, including many employees, parents, and taxpayers. Their stake in the school district is not as simple as a company's stock price. The board members themselves might be wonderful volunteers who want to do what is best for school children and the community, or they might be disgruntled former employees who want to settle a score with an administrator. One never can be certain who the community will elect to be the superintendent's boss. Nor can a superintendent be certain that the same people who participated in hiring will be on the board a year after the contract is signed. As far as compensation, there is no comparison with the private sector. The school district CEO might make three to four times what the average teacher makes, and the average teacher doesn't make nearly enough. Oh, and by the way, if you make too much, the community may just hate you for it.

Nor is it clear that a board of education actually knows what it wants. I am sure that every board wants lower taxes, higher student achievement, a happy community, hardworking but grateful teachers, well-behaved students, and exactly the right number of weather-related closings so as not to upset spring break. They want a visionary superintendent who is an instructional leader, with financial acumen, capable of sharp but not upsetting negotiating, who will live in the community, participate in church and civic affairs, make wonderful speeches, be approachable to faculty, staff, and community, and charm all comers with wit and wisdom.

In my experience, some boards are right behind their superintendent as long as it's not unpopular to do so, at which point they may still be behind the superintendent, just further behind — in fact so far behind that when the superintendent turns to make sure they are still there, they are nowhere to be found.

Litchka, Polka, and Calzi provide a great service to aspiring and practicing school leaders by exposing the "horns of dilemmas" that are often inherent in school-based decision-making. This can be more complex than increasing profit margin, though no one is oversimplifying the work of the private sector. The library aide you lay off could be a board member's wife. Moving band to the middle of the day might cause the band director to rebel, and the director might have more political capital than the principal. Block scheduling might be the right idea, but not if it disrupts some powerful employees. Buying the right house for your family that is not in the school district could be the wrong decision in the eyes of the board, even though everyone agreed it was not going to be an issue.

The dream job can become a nightmare in no time.

So how does the superintendent avoid catching a horn, and the ensuing damage to one's professional and personal life? Litchka, Polka, and Calzi make it quite clear that there are no guarantees, but provide valuable guidance to the new and experienced superintendent to increase chances not only to survive but to prosper. As I wrote with Mike Ford, every school leader enters a position very much in survival mode. The goal is to move out of survival into what we call the "creation phase" of school leadership, and perhaps even to become a legacy leader. Litchka, Polka, and Calzi give leaders practical advice that, if heeded with care, could facilitate that very outcome.

In the end, I still believe that the job of superintendent is the best job in any school district, but it is also the hardest job in any school district. It is full of opportunities and challenges, triumphs and tragedies. Success is based on competence and character and part of that competence is the ability to recognize and deal with what can be dark and self-interested political forces that have very little interest in what is truly best for students. Even the brightest, most able, most ethical leader can become a victim to these forces.

The matador in the ring can ultimately triumph, and realize incredible levels of fame and fortune. For the superintendent, leaving a district knowing you created better lives for its students will have to be fame and fortune enough, and indeed, that is worth the seemingly endless horns of a dilemma we all face.

This book is a great help. Litchka, Polka, and Calzi's work allows the superintendent to understand that the horns of dilemma are quite real, potentially dangerous, and present regardless of the competence and character of the superintendent. It should not deter great leaders from entering the ring, but remind them of the challenges they will face. Ultimately it serves as a guide to both the aspiring and practicing matador.

Stephen Uebbing
Professor of Educational Leadership
University of Rochester, New York
1999 New York State *Superintendent of the Year*

Preface

From a Muenster Beer Garden to the Chair of the Superintendency: Decisions Must Be Made

> When you are confounded with conflicting issues, decision-making seems like a monumental task. At such times, inspirational quotes on decision-making can give you the confidence to take the bull by the horns.
> —Anonymous

It all started at a beer garden in Muenster, Germany. The three of us were attending an international conference on educational leadership and after a day of presentations, we decided to have dinner and enjoy some fine German beer. We settled into one of Muenster's oldest Gaststätte (restaurants), which had just the traditional German atmosphere we were looking for to enjoy Wiener schnitzel and of course the beer.

Promptly and quite efficiently, a forceful but somewhat pleasant waitress presented us with a list of both local and regional beers. As we discussed which beer(s) to order, a gentleman at the adjoining table stated, "Don't order the local beer! I highly recommend the Belgian beer! And I have lived here all my life!" The waitress smirked, gave us a rather condescending look, and then exclaimed, "Let me know when you have made your final decision!"

And so, what had started as a simple decision-making process quickly turned into a new dilemma: Do we drink the local German beer, since we were, in fact, in Germany? Or do we go with the recommendation of one of the local residents? After some deep thought and discussion—which lasted about twenty minutes—we made a decision: we would try some of the local beer first and then try some of the Belgian beer as well.

What a pleasurable, entertaining experience in dilemma resolution: German beer versus Belgian beer in a Muenster beer garden with a bawdy waitress and an arena of onlookers awaiting our simple decision. And once our decision was made, they drifted off to focus on their own personal business—some seemingly pleased with our decision while others seemingly concerned that we made an inappropriate choice. But after all, it was our decision and we were going to live with it!

We enjoyed the levity of the experience and the relevance to the conference. With over seventy-five years of combined experience as school leaders in the United States, one would think that the three of us could make a decision—albeit one dealing with beer of all things—in a quicker and less "trying" manner (we were very thirsty!). But this simple yet complex decision became the genesis of a research project and ultimately this book.

The question that kept coming up at times during the week in Muenster was "Here we are with all of this experience in leadership. Why would it take us about twenty minutes to decide on which beer to buy, especially in the face of an anxious waitress and several local patrons?" This then led us to some rather "deeper" discussions of how we, as former school district leaders, made decisions that impacted the education of thousands of students and the working experiences of hundreds of district employees. We shared stories of decisions we made that worked out and those that did not.

Ironically, at the conference, one of us presented a session entitled "Living on the Horns of Dilemmas: A Study of School Leaders' Decision Making and Problem Solving" ("Kooperation in Schule und Unterrich: Implemenentationsansatze und perspekitiven") wherein he had identified twelve specific dilemmas that he had been researching and using as leadership lessons for courses he was teaching at the graduate level for both aspiring and practicing school district leaders.

As a result, a theme emerged at the conference among the three of us regarding the role of the superintendent of schools in making decisions, and how, more often than not, the superintendent was put into a "no-win" situation—a dilemma. And when this occurred, the superintendent was placed into a precarious situation in which, much like a matador facing off with an angry and wounded bull in a public arena, the sharp "horns" may inflict some professional as well as personal pain!

This book is about the dilemmas of decision-making that superintendents are faced with in this highly public and often tense context of the contemporary educational environment. During the next months following the Muenster beer garden episode, we met and developed a mixed methods research design and constructed a survey instrument to capture the frequency and impact of those twelve dilemmas upon practicing school superintendents.

By the spring of 2011 we had collected and analyzed the quantitative results from 258 superintendents from several Mid-Atlantic states. Subsequently, we began the qualitative research process that eventually resulted in the collection of professional insights and stories about contemporary leadership decision-making and coping with living on the horns of dilemmas from a number of school superintendents.

The qualitative part of this study consisted of structured interviews seeking responses from sample volunteer superintendents to the following questions:

- What were the situations that led to dilemmas while you were a superintendent?
- What were your immediate and long-term reactions to these dilemmas?
- What were the effects that these dilemmas/crises had on your family and friends?
- What skills did you use to try and overcome the dilemmas?
- What advice would you give to current and aspiring superintendents who are faced with similar dilemmas?

The responses from the superintendents of this sample population reinforced the perceptions that being a superintendent of schools or an educational leader anywhere today is challenging, time-consuming, and stressful to one's physical and emotional health as well as one's personal and family relationships (Litchka, Fenzel, and Polka, 2009). This representative sample provided valuable information about their respective decision-making and problem-solving approaches as well as their personal and professional experiences while living on the horns of dilemmas.

The stories we present in this book offer a glimpse into the dilemmas of decision-making, as seen through the eyes of school superintendents. Some of these stories are practical in nature, while others can be uncomfortable to the reader, especially those who may be new to the superintendency, or aspiring to enter the profession. In any case, it is hoped that these stories and accompanying comments will provoke reflection and dialogue on how the context of dilemmas and decision-making can not only impact school districts as a whole, but impact the professional and personal lives of school superintendents.

In this book, we attempt to balance the theory and conceptual framework of decision-making from a leadership perspective with the "lived" stories of practicing superintendents:

- Chapter 1: "On the Horns" introduces the reader to the context of dilemmas and decision-making. In the subsequent chapters, we present the following six dilemmas:
- Chapter 2: "Conflict vs. Consensus" — Is it best for the superintendent to promote collaborative decision-making rather than create dynamic tension, which may result in conflict but more meaningful resolution to issues?
- Chapter 3: "Trust vs. Change" — For the superintendent, does attempting to implement even the smallest change within the district result in suspicion of the superintendent's motives?
- Chapter 4: "Commitment vs. Compliance" — How probable is it for the superintendent to achieve support and commitment during times of change that also fosters compliance, given the bureaucratic

nature of command found in the contemporary K–12 education environment?

- Chapter 5: "Problems vs. Predicaments"—Does the public understand that issues found in education often are systemic and universal in nature, and thus not easily solved at the local level?
- Chapter 6: "Leadership vs. Management"—How critical is it for the superintendent to understand the difference between leadership and management, particularly within the context of decision-making, and also be able to practice one or the other when necessary?
- Chapter 7: "The Dilemma of Personal vs. Professional Life"—Is the cost to the superintendent's personal life too high in terms of the dilemma of the time, stress, and demands of school leadership?
- Chapter 8: "Matador de Toros!"—We conclude by using the metaphor of the superintendent performing as a *bullfighter in the public arena*. This final chapter provides suggestions, based on our research and experiences, to superintendents of how to become more effective at decision-making in the context of *living on the horns of the dilemmas*.

At the conclusion of each chapter, we provide "Voices from the Arena," which provides thoughts and reflections from both noted scholars as well as practicing superintendents that participated in our original study. Following that, we provide a list of questions for the reader to reflect upon. We think this book will help practicing and aspiring superintendents; as Albert Camus (1942) stated, "Life is the sum of all your choices and decisions."

ONE

On the Horns

Life is a constant oscillation between the sharp horns of dilemmas.
—H. L. Mencken

Imagine for a moment that you are the superintendent of schools in a very poor urban community where one of the district's high schools has been deemed underperforming for more than a decade in almost every aspect of student achievement. As the superintendent, you have pushed and prodded for change yet little seems to be working. There is push-back from the teachers' union and the school's principal, who is siding with the teachers. Pressure from the board of education, the community, and the state education department is mounting! Your latest proposal to the teachers' union to change working conditions has been rejected.

You and the board meet to decide the next step. The options are as follows:

1. Close the school and reopen it as a public charter school.
2. Replace all or most of the staff—including the principal—who are relevant to the failure of the school.
3. Enter into a contract with a for-profit organization to operate the school.
4. Turn over the operation of the school to the state.
5. Make another attempt at restructuring the school.

During the next two weeks, several board meetings are held in the privacy of executive session. At the conclusion of the final meeting, the board and superintendent agree to Option 2, in which the entire instructional staff and administrative staff will be replaced. All administrative and instructional positions will be advertised as vacant and the district will hire an entirely new staff for the upcoming school year, which is less than six months away. The next day, you as the superintendent announce

1

the decision. The following headlines appear during the next several months:

- *All Teachers Fired at High School!*
- *Teachers, Students, Parents Protest Board Firings!*
- *Teachers' Union in Court to Fight Firings.*
- *School Chief: I'm Willing to Talk!*
- *Governor, Ed Commissioner Support Local Board Decision.*
- *Teacher Firings: Is it Union-Busting or Real Reform?*
- *Board Decides to Rehire Fired Teachers—Superintendent Stunned!*
- *Teachers Reflect on Painful Lessons.*
- *Winners and Losers in Local School Saga.*
- *Future Up-in-Air for Local School Chief.*

Superintendents, similar to leaders of other organizations, must constantly make decisions; some are routine, while others have the potential to majorly impact the school district. Herbert Simon (1997) says that decision-making is the "heart of executive activity," while Peter Drucker (2006) suggested that "making good decisions is a crucial leadership skill at every level."

While many of the decisions made by superintendents (or those decisions made by the board and implemented by the superintendent) are not as controversial as the one in the scenario, decision-making from the superintendent's office often presents challenge. This challenge is not only determining what and how to decide, but considering the dilemmas involved in the process—those situations in which the options might be equally unfavorable or mutually exclusive.

In the scenario presented above, one could suggest that none of the options were very favorable and if selected, each could offer a myriad of consequences, both intended and unintended. Furthermore, once a decision was made, the results can not only have a dramatic effect on the school district's well-being but the superintendent's ability to lead.

The study of how leaders—and, in this case, school superintendents—make decisions is not a recent phenomenon. A recent search of a national bookseller's internet site found more than 10,600 books dedicated to leadership and decision-making. The same site listed more than 150 books in support of superintendents and decision-making. Notable writers such as Deming, Drucker, Hoy and Miskel, Hoy and Tarter, Simon, and Vroom and Yetton have helped to form a framework for effective decision-making.

Yet while there are numerous definitions of decision-making, several themes emanate including cognitive processes such as making a judgment, a response to a situation, making up one's mind among alternatives, choosing a course of action to take, and committing to a course of action after careful consideration.

The process of choosing one of the alternatives is critical in how it relates to leadership style and traits, biases, values, experiences, motivation, communication, and in some cases, resulting conflict. Furthermore, superintendents, as organizational leaders, must learn to become, at minimum, proficient at making prudent judgments. Learning to do this takes time and experience to reach such a standard. Even when a superintendent firmly believes that a decision is completely in the best interest of the children in the district, the impact of a decision can have unintended consequences such as superintendent survival that may or may not have been considered in advance.

In their seminal work that still resonates today, Vroom and Yetton (1973) suggested the following about decision-making at the organizational level:

> It can be argued, however, that the processes of decision-making when carried out by organizational leaders are different from the processes carried out by individuals in at least one fundamental respect. Organizational decision-making involves both cognitive and social processes. The events that intervene between the identification of a problem (or occasion for decision-making) and a solution or decision are both interpersonal and intrapersonal. It is the interpersonal or social aspects of decision-making that are of most direct relevance to processes of leadership. The leader not only makes decisions but also designs, regulates, and selects social systems that make decisions.

In other words, not only will the leader need to make a decision, but will also have to decide the extent to which followers will contribute to this process, including how much and in what way.

Researchers have submitted that there is no one way to make an effective decision, and although intuition and experience may help, it is often not enough; resolving an issue when faced with a dilemma is not always a rational process. Success depends upon the decision-maker possessing good judgment and a high level of sensitivity regarding the issue.

PORCUPINES, DILEMMAS, AND DECISION-MAKING

In 1851, philosopher Arthur Schopenhauer published a collection of his philosophical reflections, *Parerga and Paralipomena*. In one of the parables, he wrote of the dilemma that porcupines faced each year during the frigid winters of their habitats. According to Schopenhauer, the porcupines, on such days, would move as close to each other as possible in order to benefit from the collective heat and not freeze to death. However, the closer the porcupines got, the more they felt the sting of each other's quills, which made them move away from each other. Thus, the porcupines would actually move back and forward, from one to another.

Similar to the porcupines, the contemporary superintendent often faces the painful dilemma of decision-making. *Living on the Horns of Dilemmas: Superintendents, Politics, and Decision-Making* is about how superintendents, when making judgments, are often faced with uncertainty and confusion in trying to solve problems and make decisions in the best interest of the school district, particularly when the options may, in fact, be equally unfavorable or mutually exclusive.

Stephen Covey (1991), in his book *Principle Centered Leadership*, notes that leaders—in our case, superintendents—need to view classic leadership dilemmas from a different lens or paradigm. He suggests that leaders, particularly as the lead decision-maker, should reflect upon the following questions:

- How do we achieve and maintain a wise and renewing balance between work and family, personal and professional ambitions, in the middle of constant crises?
- How do we adhere to simplicity in the thick of terrible complexity?
- How do we maintain a sense of direction in today's wilderness, where well-developed road maps (strategies and plans) are rendered useless by rapid change that often hits us from the blind side?
- How can we be empowered (and empower other people) with confidence and competence to solve problems and seize opportunities, without being or fearing loose cannons?
- How do we encourage the desire to change and improve without creating more pain than gain?

This book attempts to help superintendents do just this. *Living on the Horns of Dilemmas: Superintendents, Politics, and Decision-Making* presents how superintendents not only "decide to decide" within the supercharged political environment of education in the twenty-first century, but will present the rich, real-life, close to the bone stories of superintendents within the context of facing dilemmas that ultimately may or may not alter the decision.

From our research, we have identified the following twelve dilemmas:

- *Centralized vs. Decentralized Decision-Making*: Is it better for the superintendent to centralize and ultimately control the decision-making process rather than to decentralize and empower others to assume responsibility?
- *Personal Life vs. Professional Life*: Is the personal cost too high for the superintendent in terms of the dilemma with one's own family issues while trying to meet the time and stress demands of school leadership?
- *Truth vs. Varnished Truth*: Is it sometimes better and more humane for the superintendent to tell a half-truth than the whole truth to

protect the interests and well-being of faculty and school site administrators, as well as the district as a whole?

- *Creativity vs. Discipline of Thought*: Is it possible to provide greater latitude of freedom for some school building leaders and still maintain structure for others who need such within a climate of collegiality?
- *Trust vs. Change*: Does implementing even the smallest organizational change result in suspicion of the superintendent's motives?
- *Leadership vs. Management*: How critical is it for the superintendents to understand the difference between leadership and management, and be able to put into practice one or the other when necessary?
- *Long-term Goals vs. Short-term Results*: How critical is it for superintendents' job security to focus on short-term improvements in areas such as student test scores rather than implementing comprehensive quality student-centered programs?
- *Motivation vs. Manipulation*: Is the superintendent authentically motivating teams to accomplish district goals rather than manipulating teams to get the results deemed most appropriate for the superintendent's success and survival?
- *Independence vs. Dependence*: Does the superintendent readily and too often accept the role of the district problem solver and decision-maker rather than facilitate others to solve their own problems?
- *Conflict vs. Consensus*: Is it best for the superintendent to promote consensus in decision-making rather than to create dynamic tension that may result in conflict but more meaningful resolution to issues?
- *Commitment vs. Compliance*: Is it possible for the superintendent to achieve commitment during times of change that foster compliance given the bureaucratic nature and hierarchical chain of command found in contemporary education?
- *Problems vs. Predicaments*: Is the public able to understand that several critical contemporary educational problems are really systemic predicaments that are more universal in nature, and not easily solved at the local level?

Consider the following story, based upon a conversation with a practicing superintendent, which offers examples of the dilemmas described that superintendents often face:

> Bernard was an educator with more than three decades of experience, including the last twelve years as a superintendent of schools for three different districts. Bernard considered himself a collaborative leader, who sought other people's opinions and consensus when making decisions that were, as he put it, "important but not urgent." According to Bernard, this collaborative style was very useful in strategic planning,

budget development, district professional development, and, of course, curriculum and instruction initiatives.

During the first year in his current district, Bernard reached out to many stakeholder groups, including parents, staff, and community organizations. He invited groups to have lunch with him, and made himself available to speak with groups throughout the community. Bernard had developed a very good working relationship with the leadership of the teachers' union. They had monthly meetings and both Bernard and this group worked very hard at resolving issues before they became serious. This collaborative style was very different from his predecessor and was welcomed by the teachers' union.

Yet Bernard, in his second year of this third superintendency, found himself in a dilemma when a decision was made "on his behalf" and he was told to "get it done sooner rather than later." Under the current contract with the teachers' union, teachers did not have to contribute to their health insurance premiums. The contract, which was for five years, was agreed to by the board of education several months prior to Bernard becoming superintendent.

The board, facing a contentious budget process, had decided to have teachers contribute 10 percent for their health insurance premiums, beginning in the new fiscal year, and that Bernard was to take the lead on this. The board also instructed Bernard to let the union know that if they did not agree to this, then significant teacher layoffs would occur in the quest for keeping the budget increase no higher than the current rate of inflation. He was also told to come up with an estimated number for layoffs if the union did not agree to this.

Bernard was stunned. He knew that the union would vehemently oppose this and all of the relationship building and collaboration that had been developed and nurtured would end immediately. Furthermore, he always felt that during times of potential budget shortfalls, the first cuts should always be as "far away from the classroom as possible." At minimum, he felt the board should have consulted with him. Of course, there would be outcry from parents who will be lamenting the fact that teacher layoffs will increase class size and ultimately have a negative effect on their child's education.

As Bernard pondered his next steps, it was clear to him that he was facing a situation in which decisions had been made, he was expected to carry them out, yet in his mind, the options for him were both limited and unfavorable from every perspective.

By far the most common perception of decision-making is one in which rational thinking occurs, when a familiar set of procedures are put into place, and concepts such as available options, expectations, preferences, and consequences are addressed by those charged with making the decision. As many leaders ultimately discover, this rational approach to decision-making does not guarantee a positive outcome, as no one can predict how others will respond to a decision, either before or after the decision has been made.

Nor can it be assumed that the decision-makers have the capabilities to create and explore an exhaustive list of options when addressing the issue. In the case of Bernard, did the board of education list and discuss every option available to resolve the impending budget problem? Furthermore, did the board have access to all relevant information?

And finally, what was the level of communication among board members when complex and specialized information and data had been discussed? Thus, the rational approach to decision-making often turns into irrational thinking and acting, and creates further dilemmas for those in charge of implementing decisions. And what may appear to be rational and clear thinking based upon consensus of those involved may actually result in conflict and chaos, landing right on the desk of the superintendent.

Yogi Berra, the baseball Hall of Fame member and sometime philosopher, once said, "If you come to a fork in the road, take it." Decision-making is often perceived as looking at options—in Yogi's example, two options—and selecting one. The dilemma, at first glance, appears to be selecting which road to take. But what happens when a superintendent, for example, faces the dilemma of having options to select that may be personally and/or professionally unfavorable to a certain degree? To further complicate this, superintendents, as we shall see, are often placed in the dilemma of implementing a decision made by the board of education that they (a) do not agree with, and (b) know will cause more harm than good to the well-being of the school district.

TWO

Conflict vs. Consensus

> When we make decisions by consensus, we are not allowed to "re-solve" conflict prematurely by choosing one thing or another. Instead we are required to hold the tension until it has a chance to open us up to a larger synthesis.
> —Parker Palmer

During the past several decades, a more collaborative approach to school district leadership has evolved in which the superintendent is encouraged to communicate effectively, bring about consensus, and make decisions that will please the board of education *and* various stakeholder groups (read: teacher unions, parent groups, and community leaders), as well as improve the quality of education. As Palmer posits, conflict—as a positive—is an integral part of this process as it helps to encourage debate, discussion, and reflection.

However, the issue facing the superintendent is: Can a process that takes more time and cause more tension be ultimately healthy for the school district or cause others to think less of the superintendent's ability to make decisions?

Consider what Miller (1984) suggested about leadership and decision-making:

Who Was That Masked Man?
Problems were always solved the same way. The Lone Ranger and his faithful companion come riding into town. The Lone Ranger, with his mask and mysterious identity, background, and life-style, never becomes intimate with those whom he will help. His power is partly in his mystique. Within ten minutes the Lone Ranger has understood the problem, identified who the bad guys are, and has set out to catch them. He quickly outwits the bad guys, draws his gun, and has them behind bars. And then there was always that wonderful scene at the end. The helpless victims are standing in front of their ranch or in the

9

town square marveling at how wonderful it is now that they have been saved, you hear hoof beats, then the William Tell overture, and one person turns to another and asks, "But who was that masked man?" And the other replies, "Why, that was the Lone Ranger!" We see Silver rear up and with hearty "Hi-yo Silver," the Lone Ranger and his companion ride away. It was wonderful. Trust, justice, and the American Way protected once again.

What did we learn from this cultural hero? Among the lessons that are now acted out daily by managers (leaders) are the following:

- There is always a problem down on the ranch (school) and someone is responsible.
- Those who get themselves into difficulty are incapable of getting themselves out of it. "I'll have to go down there and fix it myself."
- In order to have the mystical powers needed to solve problems, you must stay behind the mask. Don't let the ordinary folks get too close to you or your powers may be lost.
- Problems get solved within discrete periodic time units and we have every right to expect them to be solved decisively.

These myths are no laughing matter. Anyone who has lived within or close to our corporations (or schools) knows that these myths are powerful forces in daily life. Unfortunately, none of them bears much resemblance to the real world.

Miller presents an intriguing dilemma of the culture of leadership, where some feel that the superintendent of schools must *always* make definitive decisions, have *all* of the answers *all* of the time, model the behavior that he is *in charge*, not take too much *time* in coming to a decision, and make sure that most, if not all, decisions are *correct*. And if he can't do these, then perhaps—as a number of superintendents have found—someone else can!

While there is much in the educational leadership literature regarding collaborative leadership, perhaps the most prominent call can be found in the *Educational Leadership Policy Standards: ISLLC 2008*, adopted by the National Policy Board for Educational Administration (CCSSO, 2008). This document describes the standards and functions necessary to be an effective educational leader. Accredited educational leadership programs in universities across the nation use these standards as a foundation for their programs. Perusing these standards, one notices terms such as *shared and supported, collaboratively develop, culture of collaboration, distributed leadership, build and nurture relationships, reflective practice,* and *transparency* as they relate to educational leadership.

These abilities that the board is seeking in its next superintendent lend itself to a collaborative and open style of leadership, particularly when making decisions. Having more people involved in this process allows for an increase in the amount of information being shared and the ability of group members to better understand each other's knowledge, exper-tise, and interests. Additionally, a variety of opinions and options can be generated by the members, as well. If a group works together and even-tually comes to a consensus on a decision, there is a much better chance of support by all those involved.

However, this process can lead a superintendent face-to-face with a decision-making paradox: conflict and consensus-building (e.g., Does the board really want someone like this or is this just a way to attract certain types of applicants?).

On one hand, it would make sense for a superintendent to encourage discussion and debate in order to obtain a deeper understanding of the issues faced in making a decision. Referred to as *cognitive conflict* (Jehn, 1995), effective decision-making can occur when members exchange ide-as and information, and reflect upon their own ideas as well as others'.

For example, a superintendent has been asked by the board of educa-tion to examine whether the middle school concept is, in fact, the best way to educate adolescents. He is charged with the task to ultimately decide (recommend) if this concept should continue in the district. The superintendent could bring in educational scholars, state education offi-cials, teachers, school administrators, parents, and students to discuss this issue. Meetings could be arranged in which research could be pre-sented, data analyzed, and positions explored. During the meetings, the superintendent (or facilitator) would encourage discussion and debate by using techniques such as dialectical inquiry (Cosier and Schwenk, 1990) or consensus building.

On the surface, this type of discussion would enhance the decision-making process in that multiple perspectives are presented, discussed, evaluated, synthesized, and reflected upon. Furthermore, participants may feel that they are not only part of the solution, but may be more supportive in its implementation.

However, there are costs to this process. First, this approach takes much more time than the traditional Lone Ranger approach to making decisions. Secondly, in the contemporary educational environment, superintendents often are faced with a demanding school board and/or a public that may want immediate answers and resolutions to problems.

Furthermore, participants—including the superintendent—involved in intense discussions and debates could begin to disagree over issues that are perceived as personal and emotional. As a result, some members may respond in a way that others in the group may perceive as being overly sensitive, defensive, illogical, or negative.

Hammond, Keeney, and Raiffa (1998) offer interesting insights into "hidden traps" that can impact decision-making, particularly when it involves groups. The authors suggested, "The higher the stakes of your decision, the higher risk of getting caught in thinking trap. Worse, these traps can amplify one another—compounding flaws in reasons." They define traps as "distortions and biases — a whole set of mental flaws — that sabotage our reasoning." Listed below are the traps that leaders, such as superintendents, can fall into when attempting to have consensus-based decision-making:

- Anchor: emphasis is placed on the initial discussion; options or information, such as an incident that occurred in the past should determine how the group proceeds. *We really should have more AP classes in our high school since we never had many to begin with.*
- Status Quo: favoring options that support the current conditions or status quo. *We have always had one high school . . . we know it's large, but we can't have two smaller schools . . . it's not what this community is about.*
- Sunk Costs: favoring choices that justify previous commitments and resources, regardless if they have been successful or not. *Look, we have spent the past ten years with K–5 schools, why on earth would we divide them into primary and intermediate schools . . . look at the time and expenses we put into changing from K–6 schools and junior highs to K–5 schools and middle schools.*
- Confirming Evidence: looking for evidence that supports an existing point of view. *I called six districts who all said they would never privatize their school lunch program.*
- Forecasting: making judgments, estimates, or predictions about future events in which we have little evidence or control, and little training in (unlike weather forecasters or stock analysts). *We need to move very slowly with this ESOL initiative . . . this immigration wave from Mexico will not continue.*

As the leader, the superintendent often tries to balance both consensus and conflict in trying to make effective decisions in an efficient manner. Sometimes, though, it is more difficult to manage *agreement* rather than disagreement. Harvey (1988) refers to this as *The Abilene Paradox*, in which a decision(s) is made and on the surface, there is consensus. But below the surface, just the opposite has occurred:

- All the members agree to the nature of an issue that needs to be decided upon.
- All the members agree to the steps that need to be taken to resolve the issue.
- Individual members, however, fail to communicate their real beliefs about the issue and how to resolve it. Either no information is shared or inaccurate information is shared by the individual members.
- Actions taken lead to results that are not in the best interest of the group and its organization.

- Frustration, anger, dissension, and dissatisfaction develop, and individual members form alliances based on their real common feelings. These groups then begin to blame the leadership and other individuals within the original group for the lack of success.
- If the group members do not resolve this issue, it will repeat itself again, with more intensity.

It appears that, for whatever reasons, members of the group—including the leader—do not wish to share their *real* feelings about the issue and process. An individual member of the group may think that their own beliefs are contrary to everyone else's and he does not want to be perceived as an obstructionist or someone who "thinks differently." In reality, if everyone in the group feels the same way—and does not share these feelings—then the decision-making process will head in the wrong direction.

For example, a subordinate to the superintendent, such as an assistant superintendent, may decide *not* to be involved in the discussion for fear of reprisal from the superintendent or other members of the group. In fact, the superintendent may avoid sharing her *real* feelings about the issue for the same reasons.

Sometimes, there will be much discussion and debate regarding a particular decision that must be made. In this case, personalities and emotions dominate the discussion, and ultimately distract the group from the issue itself and how to effectively decide. Whether it is individual motives, competition, rewards/sanctions, or personal perspectives, this *affective conflict* (Jehn, 1995; Simons and Peterson, 2000) can have a negative impact on decision-making.

Since personalities and emotions dominate discussion, individual group members may become just as emotional, or decide not to become involved in the debate. Either way, the framing of the issue will be distorted and the quality of the decision diminished. Thus, there will be fewer acceptances of the final decision, and its implementation, ultimately will have a negative effect on organizational performance.

Thus, in attempting to use a collaborative decision-making model, the superintendent can be faced with a paradox of knowing that the more he involves others in the discussion of the issue at hand, it may also weaken the ability of the group to work together. In many cases, the more choices and options that are made available, the more difficult it may be to make a decision. Thus, this could lead superintendents to resort back to the Lone Ranger style of decision-making (or be forced back to it by outside influences) and have less collaboration, even though the research is clear on its overwhelming benefits.

SUPERINTENDENT'S STORY: HURRY UP, SLOW DOWN, OR ELSE!

Belle Isle is an island community of about 40,000 residents, situated between two industrial cities in the northeast. The island itself, shaped like an olive, is a little more than thirty square miles and splits the Belle River at both the north and south ends of the island. Prior to the 1960s, Belle Isle had been primarily an agricultural region, known for its many groves of lush apples, peaches, and grapes. For most of the twentieth century, the island's population had hovered around three thousand residents, mostly farmers.

To gain access to the island, there was one two-lane bridge at the south end of the island that had been built in 1925. Some residents used the bridge to commute to the city to the south, and others, from the surrounding area, used it to come to the island for the apples, peaches, and grapes (particularly during the late summer, early autumn harvest season). The Isle—as it was commonly referred to—had managed to remain a quaint, rural community.

This abruptly changed in 1962, when the state (against the vehement protests of the island residents) built two four-lane bridges: one at the east end of the island, the other at the west end, connected by the interstate highway system. The old south-end bridge was then demolished.

By the end of the decade, the population of Belle Island had surged to more than thirty thousand residents, with an influx of mostly middle-class families. These folks had kept their jobs in either city, yet moved their families to the Isle. Housing developments and small shopping centers began to become a part of the landscape, yet a number of farms were able to maintain their operations.

Like many of the industrial areas of the northeast, both cities suffered loss of industry, jobs, and, subsequently, its economic base in the last decades of the twentieth century. However, Belle Isle, with its strong roots in agriculture and the emerging light industry, was able to remain somewhat vibrant during this time. Similarly, Belle Island's population was enriched in the late 1990s and early 2000s by immigrant families from Mexico and Latin America. Most of these families were attracted to Belle Island for jobs that could be found in the fruit farming industry.

The School District

The Belle Island Central School District has an overall enrollment of approximately seven thousand students. The district has one comprehensive high school, two middle schools, and four elementary schools. Student demographics fairly represent that of the island's population: 90 percent of the students are Caucasian, 5 percent Latino, and 3 percent are African American.

The district has a seven-person school board, with each member serving a three-year term, with a limit of two terms. The central office has a superintendent, an assistant superintendent for instruction, an assistant superintendent for business, and five directors who have responsibilities for transportation, facilities, athletics, special education, and technology.

The high school's administrative team has a principal and three assistant principals, while the middle and elementary schools each have a principal and one assistant principal.

The New Superintendent

Student achievement in the school district had always been much higher than the two urban districts on either sides of Belle Isle, and comparable to other districts of similar demographics in the region. However, during the first decade of the new millennium, results of standardized tests showed a decline in the levels of proficiency, particularly among minority students and students with disabilities.

By 2008, the board of education had become very concerned about how lower student achievement had become a trend, and when the long-time superintendent decided to retire in 2010, the board began an aggressive, national search for a new superintendent.

The search for the new superintendent focused on two very distinct criteria: instructional leadership and collaboration. The board hired a national search firm to help with the process and ultimately collected more than forty applications by the deadline. The search firm reviewed the applications and presented the board with fifteen possible candidates. At this point, the board deliberated and decided to interview five of the fifteen candidates.

After two months of interviews and public presentations, the board offered Dr. Sharon Higgins the position, and she accepted. Dr. Higgins had been an educator for thirty-two years, being a teacher, principal, director, and assistant superintendent before assuming the superintendency of a rural district, about sixty miles from Belle Isle. She is well liked and respected as superintendent, known for her ability to be collaborative, down-to-earth, and someone who really cares about the profession.

Initially, Sharon thought she would stay in her present position for the next several years and then, like many of her colleagues, retire and teach at a local university. However, Sharon accepted the five-year contract to be the superintendent of Belle Isle. Family, friends, and colleagues were surprised when they heard the news that Sharon had decided to become the superintendent of Belle Isle. But as Sharon said, "I wanted to see for myself if my style of leading could be successful in a situation that frankly was 180 degrees from where I had been during the past decade."

The First Two Years

Dr. Higgins spent much of her first year in Belle Isle observing how the district was structured, particularly in how decisions were being made at all levels of the organization. She also spent much time "meeting and greeting" staff, parents, community members, and even visiting every school for one full day by the Thanksgiving break.

The superintendent also made herself available to organizations within the community to come to meetings and share her thoughts about what she was learning and to address questions and concerns as well. By the spring break in late March, Dr. Higgins had, in fact, been a guest of more than a dozen such groups, including the Belle Island Chamber of Commerce, the Lions Club, the Inter-Faith Community Alliance, and the Isle Kiwanis Club.

At the board meeting in June, Dr. Higgins presented to the board what she had observed, her perspectives, and an overview of what she felt was of critical importance in moving forward. According to Dr. Higgins, she told the board that a priority should be organizing a long-term strategic improvement plan for the district that would focus on improving student achievement, aligning resources to better support improving student achievement, and increasing collaboration between the school district and its various stakeholder groups.

At this meeting, Dr. Higgins informed the board that putting together such a plan would take about twelve months to complete, but if done correctly, such a plan would be the framework for planning and decision-making for the next five years. While a couple of the board members had concerns about "having to wait a year for the plan and then another five years for it to be implemented," the board approved her request by a 6–1 vote.

Dr. Higgins immediately put together a district-wide improvement council during the summer, with the goal that the group would meet twice a month beginning in September. She had teachers, parents, administrators, community members, and even some high school seniors. It was a large group—about forty-five members—and this council would discuss major issues in the district, such as curricular initiatives, test results, planning, and so forth. By December of her second year, the council had met eight times and had really begun to identify some core issues for the strategic plan.

Dr. Higgins implemented the "fist to five" consensus model to approve proposals, which made things go slow at times, but according to her, it really helped to "dig down to the core" of a particular issue. It took some time to get people comfortable with this process, but eventually it began to work very well. Many of the team members commented favorably to Dr. Higgins that this was the first time they had ever felt really connected to the district and that someone was finally listening to them.

It was at an early meeting in January, when the issue of character education was being discussed. While each of the schools had, to a certain degree, some sort of character building program, there was not a consistent and well-articulated program throughout the district. Since the district was made up of only seven schools, Dr. Higgins thought that this could be easily developed and implemented.

However, during this meeting, a group of parents really wanted a certain character education program adopted K–12 within the district. Three of these parents' children had been bullied, to a certain extent, in school and they wanted a very strong anti-bullying, zero-tolerance program plan implemented immediately. They presented this program to the entire council and implored the superintendent to have it approved by the council immediately. As one parent said, "We cannot wait another day . . . too many students are being bullied and something needs to be done right now."

Dr. Higgins informed the council, including these parents, that she felt very strongly the council needed to stay true to its practice of having the issue presented, options listed, research completed, and then discussion, debate, and, finally, a vote for approval. While she understood the concerns of the parents, Dr. Higgins said that the first step was to organize the task force from the council, which would then go through the steps. She also mentioned that she hoped that the parents who had shared their concerns would be willing to serve on this task force.

At this point in the meeting, one of the parents stood up and yelled to the entire group:

> You don't care about my child. He's scared to death to go to school. You don't want to talk about the real issues in this district . . . just rubber stamp what she [the superintendent] wants. Just wait until it happens to your child! Test scores and textbooks mean nothing when kids are scared!

During the next several meetings, these particular parents refused to be part of the task force, nor speak at any of the meetings. They voted no on every issue, putting their fists prominently in the air, and made a show of entering each meeting together, sitting together, and saying nothing. One time, when discussing which character education program would be the best fit for the district, they got up and left the meeting early. For the rest of that year, deep discussions and debates were seriously limited. Ironically, encouraging debate ultimately led to less discussion.

About the same time, Sharon began to sense that the some members of the board were becoming impatient with this "consensus" process, which they felt took too long. Sharon explained to them numerous times about how collaborative leadership works—as she did throughout the interview process—and that part of this process included having those involved in the decision being able to really say what is on their mind.

It was later in the second year, though, when Sharon began to feel as if things were not getting better, only worse. Although the issues regarding the character education program had somewhat subsided, Sharon found that when she thought purposeful discussions were occurring, the result was, in many cases, just the opposite of what she wanted. Sharon said,

> It got to the point that these deep conversations were turning into personal attacks and emotional exchanges. And while I wasn't naïve enough to think that this would never happen, it became the norm and not the exception. I remember, for example, sitting in executive session with the board discussing whether or not we should grant tenure to a principal. We were taking a break and two board members came up to me and said, "Look, this principal does not deserve tenure, so quit trying to pad your résumé by getting on the good side of all the principals. This group stuff you're trying to do here doesn't work . . . we need decisions made . . . now go and make them.

It was at a board meeting where portions of the strategic plan were to be presented that another incident occurred. Sharon asked three members of the team—a parent, a teacher, and an administrator—to present these statements. She wanted it presented in this way to show the board and the community that these were not "Sharon's ideas," but representative statements of the group. Once the presentations had been completed, the following exchange took place in front of everyone in attendance. A board member asked each representative how they felt these statements could help the district in the future. The responses were:

> Teacher: Well, to be honest with you, I went along with this because everyone else supported it. But to me, it really is more fluff than substance. I mean, we talked and talked and talked about this, and frankly, I could not get a word in. So I just sat there for the most part and said nothing. When it came time to vote, everyone was in favor of it, so I voted yes.

> Parent: What? I can't believe you are saying this now. You had time to speak up and didn't. But then again, you just sat there with arms folded, looking bored and disinterested . . . like you had better things to do. Most of you [teachers] hardly spoke to the rest of us. We'd have been better off if you and the others weren't on this committee.

> Principal: I support these statements, but really, it took three months of meetings to get to this point. I just wonder if all the time and resources spent on this are worth it. I hope so.

For the rest of the meeting, a debate occurred among board members and the superintendent about the process used, the leadership abilities of the superintendent, and, as one board member stated, "I agree with this being fluff . . . at this rate, it will take five years to identify what the goals of the district will be . . . can't you [Sharon] do this and then present it . . . I mean how hard can that be?"

At this point, Sharon did everything she could not to lash back at the committee members who had spoken, and the board. When the board meeting was over, Sharon—as angry and frustrated as ever—left the room and went home. She vividly remembers her thoughts that evening when she arrived home:

> I don't know who I was most angry with: the board, the committee members, or myself. I could not believe what I had heard that night. What I thought would be a rational discussion of both process and product ended up being a series of personal attacks, aimed mostly at me. Here I was, trying to have collaboration and deep discussions about very important issues facing our district, and it came down to this. I think I was more stunned by what the committee members had said than what the board member said. And then I began to wonder if all of these committees and groups that we had organized for the purpose of making effective decisions through collaboration and consensus were thinking and doing the same. I mean, was my own leadership team doing this? What about the group of principals? None of these people made any eye contact with me. I felt so alone.

One of the most significant changes that have occurred in the field of educational leadership over the past several decades has been the emphasis of having school leaders—including superintendents—develop a collaborative style of leadership. This style of leadership is found in leadership standards, university curricula, state education departments, and throughout the world of educational leadership, research, and scholarship.

The days of leading a school district via the style of the Lone Ranger or "my way or the highway" have, on the surface, been replaced by building consensus and shared decision-making. At least, that is what is being taught to aspiring and current superintendents, and being sought by boards of education as they try to find their next superintendent. The ability of a school superintendent to be collaborative and a consensus-building leader does not, on the surface, appear to be an impossible task.

But if a superintendent is to really lead in this manner, several things need to be considered. First, what is the context in which the superintendent is currently? Notices of vacancies for superintendents almost always suggest that boards of education and communities want a superintendent who is collaborative, someone who is an effective listener, and of course, an effective decision-maker. But this can ultimately lead to the dilemma itself in that, while these are the qualities being sought in a superintendent, these qualities may actually work against the superintendent in being effective in this position.

Next, is this *really* how the superintendent wants or needs to lead? Is the superintendent able to lead in this type of manner? Often times, particularly in interviews or conversations, we hear school leaders say that, of course, they are collaborative leaders and that leading by consensus is foremost in everything involving decision-making.

There are many instances that boards of education, while publicly saying they want a collaborative leader in their superintendent, privately want him or her to "get things done now rather than later," and "get those test scores up." And finally, boards of education are inclined to equate such deep discussions and debate with dissension and disharmony. In any case, it does not bode well for a collaborative, intense discussion of the issues.

Nor do superintendents necessarily have the training and experiences to be collaborative in their leadership. While many, as building principals, may have had this style to one degree or another, as they made their way to central office and eventually the superintendent's chair, the idea of collaboration and reflective discussions on core issues took on less importance.

Most significant, however, is that collaborative leadership *begs* for conflict. Not in the terms of uncivil and confrontational behaviors, but conflict that creates discussion that fuels honest and soulful interaction among the participants. As Parker Palmer (2011) stated,

> When we make decisions by consensus, we cannot proceed as long as even one person feels obligated to object on practical or moral grounds. Now I listen more openly to what you have to say—listen for where I might join with you and what I might learn from our differences. Because I know we cannot move forward unless we move together. We become collaborative listeners and speakers who develop democratic habits of the heart—such as speaking one's truth openly and listening to others respectfully—habits that can make our political discourse less divisive.

For this to occur, this leader must also have the ability to create conversations that are deep, meaningful, and reflective. In its truest sense, this means that there needs to be an environment that allows everyone involved to present, consider, and debate the relative issue that may be emotional, unpopular, controversial, or scary. And this takes time. It takes time for the leader to learn and apply this style. And it takes others—staff, parents, the community, and yes, the board of education—to learn this style and apply it effectively.

Leaders constantly implore followers to "think out of the box," yet how often does this actually occur? Whether it is the factor of time or politics or fear, often times if theoretically consensus has been reached, the reality is that below the surface, there may be just the opposite of consensus or enough anger, frustration, and/or feeling of being intimidated that followers may just vote in the affirmative just so that they can leave and move on to other tasks.

Sharon later shared with us:

> I didn't say anything . . . I was so mad that I was afraid I'd say something awful and get myself fired. But when projects under my leadership became stalled by the board and others, I was made out to be the scapegoat. People were saying, "She can't make a decision without a vote"; "It will take forever for something like this to be done, and by that time, my kids will be graduated"; "I thought we hired someone to make decisions and move this district ahead."

In terms of both *conflict* and *consensus*, the superintendent may face these two in terms of needing both of them for real success in the district, yet in reality not being able to have either. For on the surface, it appears that these two concepts will work against each other, with the end result being nothing of substance gets accomplished. Thus, a superintendent may look at it from the perspective of "Which one of these should I choose at the expense of the other?"

Superintendents need to be aware that when using collaborative decision-making, it will require a complete and honest assessment of the current issue that needs to be decided, the situational factors, and the group itself. Not all decisions need to be completed in a collaborative manner, yet there are many times in which this would be most appropriate. If the outcome is consensus, acceptance, and support for the decision, then conflict and debate must be an integral part of the process. Otherwise, effective decision-making will suffer.

Thus, is it possible for a superintendent to have consensus and dynamic conflict work together for effective decision-making? The answer is, of course, yes, but the superintendent will need to have a number of factors working in his favor. First, he must have a clear and unambiguous commitment to having *both* of these being essential components of overall decision-making. As we have seen, using only one does not equate to overall effectiveness in making decisions.

Finally, the superintendent *and* the board of education must be in agreement with and have a shared commitment to having both consensus and dynamic conflict as *the* integral part of the decision-making. And it must be a public agreement, so that there is no question in the eyes of the superintendent, the board, staff, and the public that this is the way decisions are made. And finally, continuous training and assessment should occur to ensure the commitment to both concepts continues. It doesn't have to be an either/or proposition—it just seems that the current environment mandates it!

VOICES FROM THE ARENA

Scholars

- "We are what we think. All that we are arises with our thoughts. With our thoughts we make the world." (Gautama Buddha)
- "Sometimes a change does create winners and losers. Sometimes people lose status, clout, or comfort because of change. It would be naive to imagine otherwise." (Michael Fullan)
- "Every general should go the front lines. First hand reality reminds them of their original purpose." (John Gardner)
- "Group think or social conformity is the problem. As early as the sixteenth century, Francis Bacon concluded that consensus-seeking causes us to share common myths and misconceptions." (John Gardner)
- "The fear of occasional personal conflict should not deter a team from having regular productive debate." (Patrick Lencioni)
- "People don't resist change. They resist being changed." (Peter Senge)
- "Never mind the scholars. Most people don't believe in conflict; some of them only practice." (James MacGregor Burns)

Practicing Superintendents

- "Find out sooner rather than later what the non-negotiable items are." (Suburban school superintendent)
- "You need to know where the lifeboats are." (Suburban school superintendent)
- "At times you may promote conflict, not deep anxiety conflict, but just enough to get everyone's attention." (Small-city school superintendent)
- "Vote of no confidence from the teachers union after only seven months on the job." (Small-city school superintendent)
- "People, who do not play by the rules, eventually become self-destructive." (Rural school superintendent)
- "Person elected to the board came on to attack me. Trust was an issue. Personal attacks that were intended to destroy my career." (Rural school superintendent)
- "People are angry. People have to learn to work together or we are not going to survive." (Rural school superintendent)

REFLECTION

1. The education system has been under much scrutiny by the media, politicians, and special interest groups. In what ways can we exercise leadership to create a more positive image?
2. How can we ensure the expectations of the school system do not become so demanding that we overwhelm the system?
3. How do school leaders minimize the conflicts that arise due to the competing needs of special interest groups?
4. What role does your school district play to reform the system? To what extent is it necessary to have central office support? What kind of support is most needed?

THREE

Trust vs. Change

You must be the change you want to see in the world.
—Mahatma Gandhi

The senses deceive from time to time, and it is prudent never to trust
wholly those who have deceived us even once.
—René Descartes

Much is expected of our schools today and policy makers throughout the
nation have made improving education a priority. Schools, like other
social institutions, reflect the dynamics of our contemporary culture, of
which, as someone once said, "The only constant in the world is change."

Student achievement (read: raising test scores), depleting resources,
and the politicizing of education are but a few of the demands placed at
the doorstep of the superintendent's office. Superintendents are often
battered with a multitude of proposals, research, and mandates to change
the current way of educating students into "a new and better way." The
pressure on superintendents to change can be in conflict with the community's insistence on having better schools yet, at the same time, pre-
serving the traditional aspects of the community's culture.

We suggest, within the context of the dilemmas of decision-making,
that the superintendent be aware of two critical components of the
change process: first, understanding the psychology of change, and second, the importance of trust within the process. Yet as all leaders know,
trust is earned not mandated, and the change process in itself is fraught
with intrigue, politics, and agendas. Although written more than five
centuries ago, what Machiavelli (1513) suggested about leadership and
change is apropos to the contemporary superintendency:

> It should be borne in mind that there is nothing more difficult to man-
> age or more doubtful of success or more dangerous to handle than to
> take the lead in introducing a new order of things.

For the innovator has enemies in all those who are doing well under the old order, and only lukewarm defenders in all those who would do well under the new order.

The lukewarmness arises partly from the fear of their adversaries who have laws on their side, and partly from the incredulity of those who do not truly believe in new things until they have solid experience of them.

Thus it happens that whenever his enemies have the opportunity to attack the innovator, they do so with zeal of partisans, and the others only defend the innovator tepidly, so that the innovators, together with them, is put in danger.

Now, consider what one superintendent shared with us:

Everyone—the board, administrators, teachers, and parents—wanted me to be the superintendent who was, in fact, the instructional leader. And I was very comfortable doing this. Until I tried to change some of the ways things were done in the district. For example, the junior high staff was asked to look at going to the middle school concept instead of the current junior-senior high concept. And I wanted the high school staff to look at block scheduling as a means to developing a more student-centered classroom.

Now, I didn't try to do this all at once. We started studying block scheduling at the high school the first year, then studying the middle school concept the following year. In both cases, I used what I thought was a collaborative model and had a goal of two-year study and discussion before any decision was to be recommended to the board.

The resistance came from everywhere.

Teachers were protective of their own individual turfs, principals were uneasy trying to lead these potential changes, and parents were upset that this was not the way they were taught. Furthermore, I was accused more than once of "having an agenda to pad my résumé." Needless to say, neither change was made!

From this example, several interrelated concepts are evident. Leading change is difficult as is accepting change and the perceived motives of the leader in introducing change—whether real or not—play a critical role in moving the change process along. In our research, we describe this as a dilemma in the following manner: Does implementing even the smallest of change result in suspicion of your motives as a leader? The successful superintendent, therefore, needs to have both a deep understanding of change theory *and* be able to create an environment in which trust is at the forefront of all interactions.

The relationship between change theory and leadership has been a popular topic for scholars, researchers, policy makers, and practitioners for the past century. There are literally thousands of books, journal articles, manuals, and manuscripts that provide many different perspectives on this relationship. Some of the most influential writers in this area—both in and out of the field of education—include Fullan; Hersey and

Blanchard; Kotter and Cohen; Kouzes and Posner; Lewin; Marzano, Waters, and McNulty; and Senge, and they helped us to conceptualize this critical area of school leadership.

Though most superintendents are aware of change theory, the concept of trust and how it relates to the change process is of critical importance. In the contemporary educational environment, a culture of mistrust appears to dominate much of the landscape.

Considering the ever-increasing levels of standardization and accountability, teachers are not trusted to deliver appropriate instruction; parents are not trusted to raise their children appropriately; schools don't trust central administration; central administration doesn't trust the state education agency and/or the state government; and so on. In many school districts, in addressing critical issues, the toxic culture of mistrust inhibits progress, collaboration, and the implementation of effective decisions.

Being a leader in this environment is certainly not easy. Yet it is clear that building trust among and between stakeholders might be the most critical leadership strategy a superintendent can embark upon. More than two decades ago, John Gardner (1990) stated

> There is much to be gained for any leader in winning trust of constituents. A leader capable of inspiring trust is especially valuable in bringing about collaboration among mutually suspicious elements in the constituency. The trust the contending groups have for such a leader can hold them together until they begin to trust one another.

Without trust, the basics of communication—people speaking and listening—can become limited, distorted, and eventually lead to disengagement or disruptive interactions. And what makes this even more difficult for the superintendent is the fact, as mentioned above, that lack of trust and suspicion of motives may already be entrenched within the culture before any discussion of change occurs.

Patrick Lencioni submits that trust may be the most critical factor for the leader and members of the organization to have. According to Lencioni (2002),

> When it comes to teams, trust is all about vulnerability. Team members who trust one another learn to be comfortable being open, even exposed, to one another around their failures, weaknesses, even fears. Vulnerability-based trust is predicated on the simple—and practical— idea that people who aren't afraid to admit the truth about themselves are not going to engage in the kind of behavior that wastes everyone's time and energy.

Thus, if trust becomes both a core belief and core behavior within the school district and the superintendent models these beliefs and behaviors, then coherence, continuity, good faith, and fairness will more likely occur, especially during the stressful times of introducing change. In this next story, we share the dilemma of change and trust.

SUPERINTENDENT'S STORY: THE SHIFTING WINDS OF CHANGE

Michael Ricardo had a successful career as a high school principal in a small-city school district for eight years when he was approached by a consultant to apply for the superintendency at Oakville, another small-city community about sixty miles from where he and his wife and two children lived. Obviously, he was flattered he was asked to apply. His wife was supportive; they both thought he could do the job and the change would be good for their family. After all, he was convinced that leadership, whether school building or school district was still about leading people, things, and ideas and should not make a difference regardless of the position in education.

After agreeing to apply, Michael discovered that the initial slate of candidates was not accepted by the majority of the board, and it was necessary for the consultant to re-open the search. After personally interviewing potential candidates, the consultant submitted a list of five names to the board for their approval. The first step in this process included an interview with a board appointed committee.

Since this approach was new to him, he decided to meet with a highly regarded superintendent, who previously agreed to serve as his mentor. Michael was advised by the experienced superintendent to visit the community along with his wife before the scheduled committee interview.

In preparation, he gathered information about Oakville's programs, people, and reputation. He developed an interview plan, prepared a list of anticipated questions, memorized the names of as many committee participants as possible, and did as much research as could be found on the district website, including data from the state education department and the local newspaper. He was well prepared for the interview.

Subsequently, Michael was one of three candidates recommended by the committee for further consideration by the board of education. During the board interview process, each board member was given an opportunity to ask one question. The face-to-face interview with the board was limited to one hour. Michael knew that because of time limitations, he needed to be as clear and concise as possible and be able to maintain focus.

He addressed each board member by name and tried to include relevant past achievements/results without sounding arrogant. If needed, he was prepared to use a series of documents that he brought with him to support his verbal responses. He was disappointed that because of time limitations the process did not allow an in-depth dialogue with all board members so that he could get to know them better as individuals. But at the conclusion of the interview several board members asked if he would leave documents for further review.

Michael felt fortunate to be selected on a 7–0 board vote and was awarded a three-year contract renewable at the end of the second year as superintendent of schools. The contract also included family health insurance, car use, school-related conference expenses, a whole life insurance policy, a tax sheltered annuity, one month of vacation time, a liberal sick leave benefit, and a very handsome salary. And if he should retire from the school district, health insurance would continue and unused sick time would result in a one-time payment.

In addition, there was provision that if the board wanted to terminate the contract at any time, he would be paid a lump-sum severance amount equivalent to 75 percent of the remaining value of the contract. At that moment in the board meeting when the deciding vote was cast, Michael caught the eye of his wife and, smiling, both thought that life was good! Indeed, he thought, it is very good to be the superintendent of schools!

However, the smiles quickly turned to surprise when immediately after the board approved the contract, a reporter from the Oakville Star newspaper demanded a copy of his contract from the board president. Michael was now a 24/7 public figure whose actions would be scrutinized by the media and reported to the public. In this age of hyper-accountability and taxpayer concern for expenditures, Michael quickly learned that his lucrative leadership contract was not widely supported by all city residents.

There were immediate concerns expressed about the terms and conditions of his contract as well as questions about why someone like him from outside the school district should be so rewarded. Reporters questioned if Mr. Michael Ricardo was like the superintendent hired in a neighboring district a few years ago; brought in to make some key changes in district operations and then when the changes became too aggressive for the community that superintendent was simply "bought out" of his contract.

However, that superintendent was widely known in the state as the penultimate change agent or as some faculty and administrators derisively called him: "The Mercenary Superintendent": he "blows-in," "blows-up," and then "blows-out with a pocket full of our cash!" But the board members staunchly supported their collective decision to appoint him because, as they stated, "he was the best person for the job at this time given the changes that the district must endure over the next five years."

Surviving this initial issue, Michael enjoyed a very successful first year. He was able to solve several major problems dealing with personnel, contract disputes, and district funding reductions. His perception was that because of his successful experiences in making financial decisions and resolving personnel issues he had garnered enhanced respect from the members of both the Oakville Board of Education and the administrative staff.

Michael soon realized that he had to be much more sensitive in dealing effectively with people concerning various community problems as superintendent in this school district because too often they became very emotional when decisions were made, even if their input was solicited, and often would run to the media for support claiming that the school system was biased.

Michael often questioned whether or not superintendents were prepared to work with school boards who represented the community-at-large and had such diverse backgrounds, interests, and motivations. He had no idea that there was such a difference in the leadership role demands between the high school principal and the superintendent. In retrospect, he confided that he had more control as a high school principal in problem solving and decision-making than as a school superintendent. He was certified to be superintendent of schools in his state, but not necessarily as qualified as he felt he should be to deal with the public and the board of education. This position was much more political than he had anticipated or even been taught to imagine!

But Michael felt that he possessed a strong set of core values and a strong belief in effectively educating students and he was adamantly willing to take a stand against anything that undermined that belief. In his mind, school leadership was that simple. But he also wondered at times if his administrative staff and school board members felt the same way. However, he found out quickly that there were incongruities between his value system and those of others in the educational community.

During his first year, when discussing applicants for an administrative position with the board of education in executive session he was very surprised by comments made by the board president and other board members. As they were discussing the differences between the administrative candidates, the board president responded to one of Michael's questions about quality measures in the following way, "good is good enough . . . we don't need to pay to bring in the best and most highly qualified candidate." Michael then asked, "what is more important: residency or quality?" Several members of the Board responded "residency."

Michael could now feel the tension that seemed to be evolving between him and some members of the board of education. They hired him and liked the ideas about change that he espoused at his interview and they seemed to appreciate all of the good decisions he made during his first year as superintendent but now there seemed to be a growing rift in his relationship with some members of the board of education as well as with his administrative staff and teachers.

One of his administrators told him after a meeting in one of the elementary schools at the end of his first year that some people "don't trust you because you are not one of us and your history here is brief." When Michael responded to that administrator, "How long do you think it will take for them to trust me?," the administrator's response was, "One never knows."

At the start of his second year as superintendent, Michael came to the realization that with declining enrollment in the elementary schools and rising costs for building maintenance, it was time for the district to consider closing an elementary school. Spruce Elementary was the oldest elementary school of the five elementary schools in the district and yearly had the most need for maintenance and repair funds. Its enrollment was rapidly declining and the students could be sent to the other four elementary schools of the school district.

Subsequently, Michael spent the next year focusing on reducing district expenditures by eliminating one elementary school and reducing costs in other budget areas. He established an advisory committee consisting of representatives of the various stakeholders of the district and together with his administrative team and board of education liaisons they planned several open forums about the school district financial picture and the need to consolidate operations, including closing an elementary school.

Spruce Elementary School was "targeted for closure" because it was the oldest elementary school, had the most deteriorating physical conditions, and had the most rapidly declining enrollment. It most fit the "closing metric" that the advisory committee had developed. So the advisory committee prepared their report and presentation regarding their recommendation to close Spruce Elementary for the board of education meeting early in the calendar year so a smooth transition of students could be logistically developed.

Michael was satisfied that he had "all the ducks in a row" on this key budget proposal and that both the advisory committee and the administrative team backed his plan to recommend the closure of Spruce Elementary. There were only minor concerns expressed by some parents at the public forums regarding student transfers but, all in all, the plan he developed to gain community and board support for this major change had worked. All that was needed was the official board of education vote on the proposal to close and "mothball" Spruce and transfer Spruce students to the other schools using his well-developed logistical schema. The stage was set for the board to act and make the change.

Then, the local newspaper printed the following:

> Oakville—More than 500 residents were in attendance last night for the Board of Education meeting where by a 4–3 vote witnessed the Board turn down Superintendent Michael Ricardo's recommendation to close Spruce Elementary School. Students from Spruce would have been distributed to other elementary schools in the district. Sentiments ran high. Many in the crowd were in an angry mood as reflected in one sign that read "WE elected YOU to represent us not tell US what to do."

At stake in this critical decision was the potential savings in estimated expenditures per year of over $532,000, and the district would also be in jeopardy of not being able to present for public vote a budget of under a 2 percent tax levy as mandated by the state. If exceeding the 2 percent cap the district would be faced with a 60 percent voter approval in order for the budget to pass. Prior to the board vote on this issue, the public was provided with an opportunity to address the board. Some of the questions asked by parents, teachers, and community members were as follows:

Has the distribution of pupils on the west side changed considerably since the Citizens Committee Report of three years ago prior to the arrival of this new superintendent?

It appears that the school was studied for closure in order to save money. It is important to show us that closure would at a minimum result in an increase in the quality of the education. Will this be the case?

Why weren't other schools like Transit Elementary School, almost as old as Spruce, considered for closing?

What statistics are live births based upon?

Will there be a reduction of teachers who are employed?

Won't some of the redistributed students like the sixty students at Horace Mann overcrowd the general facilities at that school—the library, the cafeteria, and places for music and art?

How important is this hearing to you as members of the board of education?

Was the decision already made by YOU and YOUR superintendent prior to public forums?

Was the advisory committee just a sham because this superintendent wanted to close Spruce from the day he was hired by you?

After all of the planning and meticulous attention to community input, Superintendent Ricardo found it difficult to understand why the board voted not to close Spruce Elementary by a vote of 4–3. Although no vote or discussion was held in executive session before the public meeting and vote, every board member appeared to be in favor of his recommendation to close Spruce Elementary. Why the sudden change? Was it a lack of trust? Did he and his staff not properly develop the plan of action that supported the recommendation? Were there issues behind the scenes that he did not know or anticipate?

The questions raised at the community meeting might indicate a lack of trust. If so, what worried him most was that mean-spirited personal attacks would likely follow. He contemplated his options throughout the restless night as he returned home weary from that board meeting. He kept thinking:

> Just what are my options now? Should I ignore this situation? Should I get angrier at the board for their "sudden collapse" in the face of com-

munity pressure, but that won't make it go away! In fact, a poor temper on my part at this time may make things even worse. Wishful thinking is a waste of time, and I can't run away from the realities of this sudden rebuke by the board and community. What should I have done differently and what do I do now?

Obviously, he knew early in his superintendency that he would not be able to control situations as easily as when he was a principal. But he was irritated by the thought that the position of superintendent was not one of primarily an educational change leader and community statesman, but one overrun with power politics.

The board decision not to support his recommendation to close Spruce Elementary was a difficult one for him to personally and professionally accept. The more he reflected, the more he began to realize what went wrong. Perhaps he was at fault by not appreciating the obvious facts when he was hired. He was going to be the educator "litmus paper" test for the board of education whenever there were "hot-button" community issues to resolve. And the board would make political decisions and not follow his recommendations if they were counter to the wave of public opinion.

He even questioned his naiveté as a second-year superintendent. He began to question his ability to lead this district. Were there ways to help prevent issues such as this that end in a personal setback? Was it a question that he was driving the change on the opposite side of the road from everyone else and was he not looking in his rear-view mirrors and paying attention to what was going on behind him?

Michael knew that there always would be turmoil if he attempted to make significant changes. He accepted this conclusion as the superintendent's way of life, be it managing declining enrollment, introducing new procedures for evaluating staff, developing assessment procedures for improving the teaching/learning process, or re-configuring the school district and closing schools. These initiatives certainly would create anxiety and unrest among all educational stakeholders. Were there ways to minimize destructive anxiety and promote constructive conflict?

As a result of this school closing debacle, he decided to address the issue of trust and change within the school district. He thought that after all, "change was everyone's job and responsibility" since in the Darwinian sense "it's neither the strongest nor the fastest of the species who survive—it's those who are most adaptable" and schools, like other social institutions need to "change or die."

So he decided to discuss this topic at his administrative team meeting that was regularly scheduled the morning after every board of education meeting. He felt strongly that the team was either part of the solution or part of the problem. He wanted to emphasize that mastering change is increasingly every school administrator's job and that everyone including himself needed to know how to successfully guide people through the change process.

Yet this meeting presented additional surprises to him. The administrative staff was equally divided. And he quickly realized that patience was critical even though he always felt a sense of urgency in discussing educational changes. He needed to tread softly as some of the administrators were obviously shaken by the community's show of power, whereas others seemed to be content that the community had spoken.

Michael started this meeting by identifying that perhaps he should have spent more time helping people, particularly staff members, to become more aware of the need for change to reduce district expenditures. But one of the senior administrators said, "It didn't matter, that community doesn't trust you and by association, they don't trust most of us! Many of them have voiced the opinion that you are nothing more than a 'hired gun' out to make changes and then move on like others in the region have done. They don't feel your sense of commitment to their community or school district and they believe your school closing and other changes you advance that impact them are simply designed to further 'marginalize them' and maintain the power status quo in this district!"

Michael was now convinced, more than ever, that as a school leader in the most demanding position in the school district, his role was to create a meaningful transformation in this school district: a transformation of values, actions, economics, and procedures. He knew that he could maintain "what is" through his position, but sustainable changes, those that challenge the status quo, had to begin with the support of staff and a trust in him to do the right things to them, by them, and for them.

If he expected to achieve positive sustainable changes in this district, he would be involved in inevitable controversy at every step of the change journey: How could he do that and still convince the educational community to "trust" that he was promoting these changes for their good?

Michael Ricardo maintained his composure to this personal assault at this meeting and accepted the admonishment as a catalyst to take a more focused approach to developing personal relationships with his administrative staff, school faculties, and, most assuredly, the renegade board of education as well to become more involved in the entire community.

He also accepted the fact that dynamic tension is the life blood of living as a superintendent. He thought that some stressful moments between he and the board may, at times, be useful and produce better results. Also, he began to feel that maybe it was unnecessary to worry over the magnitude or number of problems he faced, as conversations with other superintendents identified, since these were endemic to leading schools.

In this chapter, we have focused on the dilemma of trust and change. We have found that when handling a "dilemma within the dilemma," it appears trust and change pull in opposite directions. Leading a school district through a change of significance is never an easy task, but it appears to be even more daunting when these two critical factors are not in harmony.

Despite enormous amounts of research, programs, resources, and energy, implementing change within school districts has not been successful, especially in those districts that are in need of the most reform. Sometimes, school boards want to hire a leader who can be *the* change agent, yet due to many factors, the board does not provide support, time, and resources for the changes to be developed, implemented, and monitored. On the other hand, a superintendent may come into a district with a preconceived plan of what changes need to occur, how the changes will occur, and when these changes occur, well before learning about the district's needs, wants, and resources.

We do know, however, that effective leadership is a key to having a successful change process occur in a school district, including leadership from the board and from faculty, staff, and the community. But the key to successful reform and change initiatives is the quality of leadership the superintendent provides throughout the process.

While there is no one style of leadership that guarantees success in implementing change, the ability of the superintendent to communicate this initiative to all the stakeholders is critical, as is the ability to collaborate, build consensus, and create a sense of urgency and energy that will enhance the chances of success.

The critical question regarding change and trust is the proverbial: Which comes first? On the surface, it would appear logically that a superintendent needs to first develop a sense of trust among those with whom he or she will be interacting. But building trust takes time, and as we saw in the previous story, school boards and communities often do not allow the superintendent the time to develop relationships and trust. Furthermore, if trust has not been developed, it is rather easy for the school board, staff, faculty, and/or the community to question the motives of the superintendent in pressing for such change.

Throughout our observations and interviews, we heard many comments from superintendents regarding the dilemma of trust versus change, which resonated with the literature in this area of leadership. What they were saying had an uncanny alignment to what scholars in leadership have been stating for quite some time. A sampling of contemporary leadership literature that we used in the development of our research regarded both the change process and trust, and what the superintendents shared with us appears at the end of this chapter.

From the comments expressed by practicing superintendents during our interview process and along with what has been found in the literature, one wonders if trust and change can work together. We believe so, but why doesn't it work very often? Some may say that boards of education are impatient and may not really trust the superintendent. Boards may question the motives of the superintendent, or may be under pressure from the community to *speed things up but don't go too fast.*

On the other hand, perhaps it may be that the superintendent is, in fact, impatient and perhaps does not really trust the board of education, or the superintendent may lack the attributes and skills to get the job done. The superintendent may be questioning the motives of individual members of the board, or the entire board itself. And the superintendent may be under pressure from staff, teachers, and the community to "change but not too much and not without our consent."

It is no secret that implementing change within an organization is extremely difficult, dangerous, and stands a good chance of not succeeding—even if "all of the stars and moons are in alignment." And if things go awry, we can be sure that most, if not all, of the blame will be aimed at the superintendent. After all he is the point person and considered by many to be the last word. And if these statements have a certain amount of truth in them—and we often believe they do—then what can a superintendent do when he or she thinks a significant change is necessary, or if the board and/or community is pressuring for a substantial change?

We submit, on the basis of how treacherous change can be, that trust is the key to this dilemma. First of all, if there is a lack of trust between the superintendent and board of education (or staff, teachers, community, etc.), most likely nothing of substance—including a proposed change—will occur. Secondly, building trust is a process for all parties to understand and appreciate each other, get to know each other, and accept each other—especially if the superintendent is new to the school district or there has been a dramatic change in the makeup of the board of education.

As with the literature regarding change, there is much in leadership about the critical nature of trust and its impact on the success or failure of a leader. We know, for a fact, that trust takes time to build and not much time to have it lost. Perhaps it takes the willingness of the superintendent and school boards to not accept the existing models of how to define leadership, how to improve schools, and how to build sustainability within the swirling vortex of the contemporary educational environment.

Therefore, the first order of business for a superintendent and the board is to begin a formal process of building trust through trustworthy actions, not just letting it develop on its own. We believe it has to be purposeful, strategic, collaborative, and different from the existing models.

In summary, the key word for resolving the trust versus change dilemma is leadership. A school leader considered trustworthy is one who actually practices value based leadership. As part of this leadership agenda, it must be a person who can also manage the work of others by developing a plan of action that is well conceived and essential for motivating and gaining a critical mass of support. It means taking the ideas and concepts off paper and implementing them. It is why a school district staff with a strong culture comes to work each day to build, to lead, to change in the quest for continuous improvement in the school district.

Throughout our observations and interviews, we heard many comments from superintendents regarding trust versus change, which resonated with the literature in this area of leadership. What they were saying had an uncanny alignment to what scholars in leadership have been stating for quite some time. The following provides a sampling of contemporary leadership literature that we used in the development of our research regarding both the change process and trust, and what the superintendents shared with us.

FROM THE ARENA

Scholars

- "Moral purpose is about both the ends and means. In education, an important end is to make a difference in the lives of students." (Michael Fullan)
- "Yesterday's solutions for improving schooling may be insufficient for tomorrow's children." (Francis Duffy)
- "Understanding the change process is less about innovation and more about innovativeness. It is less about strategy and more about strategizing." (Michael Fullan)
- "Rules almost always protect the status quo. Rules tend to protect self-interest." (Francis Duffy)
- "Successful educational reform ultimately requires a broad and sustainable coalition of support, and the route to this goes directly through, and not around politics." (Clarence Stone)
- "We should reconcile ourselves to the fact that nothing in the world is entirely positive; power can be misused. Love may lead to cruelty, science can create destruction, and technology unchecked produces pollution." (Mihaly Csikszentmihalyi)
- "This is why close relationships are not ends in themselves. Collaborative cultures, which by definition have close relationships, are indeed powerful, but they are focusing on the right things they may end up powerfully wrong." (Michael Fullan)
- "The greatest impact on an organization will come from technologies 'outside' its own field." (Peter Drucker)
- "Authentic school leaders do not necessarily champion a 'my way or the highway' philosophy, but they are unwilling to sacrifice their

priorities and goals, and when necessary they will challenge those who can't or won't go along." (Robert Evans)

- "To 'control' everything is to control nothing. And to attempt to control the irrelevant always misdirects." (Peter Drucker)
- "Trust is the emotional glue that holds teams together." (Tichy and Bennis)
- "Exemplary leaders always seem to be present when there is a search for opportunities to introduce the new and untried. Leaders may be rule makers, but they are also rule breakers." (Kouzes and Posner)
- "The key to all of this [establishing trust] is involving team members on establishing norms, and then having everyone holding each other accountable . . . the fear of personal conflict should not deter a team from having productive debate." (Patrick Lencioni)
- "Learning to lead is thus not simply a matter of style, of how-to, of following some recipe, or even mastering 'the vision thing.' Instead leadership is about ideas and values. It is about understanding the differing and conflicting needs of followers. And it is about energizing followers to pursue a better state [goal] than they had thought possible." (James O'Toole)

Practicing Superintendents

- "There is a need to know what your core beliefs are." (Suburban school superintendent)
- "Every child—and I mean every child—has a right to a quality education . . . and if that is not happening in our district, then we will change!" (Small-city superintendent)
- "The job is not about having the right answers but really, about asking the right questions." (Rural superintendent)
- "It took four years before things started to come together . . . much longer than I ever thought." (Suburban superintendent)
- "Listen! Listen! Listen! It is 50% of the communication process." (Small-city superintendent)
- "As a new superintendent, my biggest mistake was that I thought—hell, I'm the superintendent, they should just do what I say. What I should have done was build up some support and relationships." (Small-city superintendent)
- "Superintendents must possess a well-established philosophy. You need to spend time reflecting and continuing to work hard on its implementation." (Urban superintendent)
- "At times, you need to promote conflict, not deep anxiety . . . just enough to get everyone's attention." (Small-city superintendent)

- "My favorite question . . . which by the way drove everyone nuts from day one . . . why are we doing it this way? Help me understand, that's all!" (Urban school superintendent)
- "I was able to make changes in a short time, able to do so because they were the same changes recommended seven years ago during the tenure of another superintendent." (Urban school superintendent)
- "I knew we had to make changes . . . so the first thing I did was change some of the ways that people perceive the superintendent . . . so I changed the way we had meetings, when we had meetings . . . one time I even had a meeting where we all stood throughout the meeting." (Rural school superintendent)
- "A strong core of people in the city did not trust the authority . . . the board, the superintendent . . . and without it [trust] we could not move one step forward." (Small-city superintendent)
- "The greatest dilemma was a lack of trust when change was needed the most." (Rural school superintendent)
- "My business administrator was a direct line of communication to some of the board members . . . when I discovered this, I could never trust him again and, frankly, the district suffered because of it." (Suburban school superintendent)

REFLECTION

1. What lever is powerful enough to usher in trust and change?
2. Name a variety of ways a school leader can communicate their core values.
3. Since a school leader is dependent upon a level of involvement of one's followers, how does the leader engage passive followers to become active followers?
4. What core processes do we need to put in place in our day to day practice as school leaders?

FOUR

Commitment vs. Compliance

Power and political behavior used in negative ways are often effective in the short term but ineffective in the long term. In the short term, negative power creates compliance not commitment. Compliance creates immediate action by the leader. Commitment, on the other hand, motivates people to do what's best for a school district without being forced to do so. Commitment trumps compliance, because commitment creates long-term positive outcomes.
—Francis Duffy, 2006

It is difficult to read or observe the media today without noticing a headline or commentary related to the quality of education in America. According to some, drastic change is urgent and important. Since the passage of the No Child Left Behind Act in 2002, federal involvement in local school districts has increased dramatically. The purpose of the law was to improve the academic achievement of all students by setting higher standards, increasing accountability through mandated annual testing, ensuring adequate progress, and finally through imposing rewards and penalties.

What then are the options for those school districts that have consistently demonstrated over the past decade that student achievement *in their district* far exceeds the standards set by NCLB legislation? Should these schools be "painted with the same brush" as those districts who, for whatever reasons, have not met the standards?

In this chapter, we present the dilemma of commitment versus compliance. Superintendents are often faced with this dilemma when making decisions and/or solving problems, since on one hand, having the people within the organization committed to an effort will most likely lead to a better chance for success.

However, on the other hand, superintendents may have to be more autocratic in moving an idea forward. What can compound this dilemma is if the superintendent is finding resistance to an idea, yet is in no position to not comply with the mandate, whether it comes from the federal government, state education agency, or even the local board of education. Or as we shall see in this chapter's story, what if the superintendent must legally comply with a mandate, yet the board of education, due to pressure from the community, refuses?

Many writers in educational leadership suggest that, historically, school districts have been operating for the most part on the nineteenth-century hierarchical, organizational model. However, as Michael Fullan (2001) states, "In hierarchical systems, it is easy to get away with superficial compliance or even subtle sabotage." Referred to in terms such as authoritative leadership, autocratic leadership, or control leadership, writers such as McGregor, Maslow, Covey, Collins, and Senge have been critical of this type of leadership for organizations. They argue that this emphasizes power, control, and where success is determined by the leader's agenda—who in turn, sets goals, strategies, rewards/punishments, and control.

In fact, Collins (2001) suggests that this type of leader often spends an inordinate amount of time and resources "conspiring" to have the followers in the organization "buy into what is being sold" (comply) as something that will be good for the individual as well as the entire organization. Most times, just the opposite happens in that there is little if any acceptance, or if so, only because of the nature of authority and control over rewards/punishments.

Furthermore, it can be posited that if the organization is interested in long-term, sustained growth, the leader will have less chance of success by using authoritative means. Compliant leadership seldom allows an organization to move ahead. As Collins and Hansen (2011) state, "compliant leadership cannot generate the passion to move an organization from good to great." Leaders using these strategies are unlikely to find problems being solved and decisions being made that are in the best interest of the organization.

Fullan (2006) states, "The litmus test of all leadership is whether it mobilizes people's commitment to put their energy into actions designed to improve things. It is individual commitment, but is above all collective mobilization." As we have mentioned, school districts need—or at least say they need—leaders who can collaborate with stakeholder groups, communicate effectively, and create a synergy within the district that is inspiring, passionate, and committed to excellence. And the key may be in the ability of the superintendent to be committed to excellence, and be able to generate such a commitment throughout the organization—not by merely forcing people to comply.

As we have seen in education during the past decade, schools have been forced to "comply" with the very strict models of success or failure, based upon the input-output model. Thus, compliance leadership often becomes a critical factor for a superintendent in moving a district in a particular direction, even if the superintendent considers himself or herself to be a collaborative leader.

Over time, much work in leadership has been completed that strongly suggests that a more collaborative type of leadership is much more effective than the compliant model described above. Collins describes this type of leadership as "Level 5 Leadership," in which the leader brings passion to the organization, but leaves his ego outside.

Another example is the work of Kouzes and Posner (2007), who have developed a leadership model based upon five practices of exemplary leaders. Each of the five practices presented in this model (Model the Way, Inspire a Shared Vision, Challenge the Status Quo, Enable Others to Act, Encourage the Heart) relate back directly to what the authors say is the first law of leadership: "If you don't believe the messenger, you won't believe the message." They suggest that the practice of Model the Way aligns directly to the concept of trust and credibility. The leader is very clear in clarifying personal and organizational values, and then behaving in a manner that is an example for others to follow: "People trust the leader when their deeds and words match."

SUPERINTENDENT'S STORY: NO CHILD LEFT UNTESTED

Gwen Osterberg had a distinguished career as a teacher, building administrator, and assistant superintendent for curriculum and instruction, as well as superintendent of schools. Throughout her career she had worked on and managed several curriculum projects for the state education department designed to promote more excellence and equity for all students. Gwen was well respected not only in her region but also statewide and had many colleagues both at the school district level and statewide who endorsed her as she advanced into more comprehensive and prestigious leadership roles.

Gwen truly believed and practiced constructivism and always focused her efforts on individualizing instruction so that all students could achieve to their fullest potential. She was very much a student-centered educator who put "children first" when making administrative decisions, and was known for sage advice and counsel about curriculum and instruction to state education officials and colleagues. Gwen consistently advocated that if administrators "made decisions based on doing what is in the best interest of students that they would, in fact, be doing the right thing for the right reasons."

However, it was during her third superintendency that Gwen faced a major dilemma related to her professional commitment to both school district constituents and compliance with state regulations related to student standardized testing.

Gwen was appointed superintendent of schools of the prestigious Southpointe Heights Central School District, one of the top performing and wealthiest school districts in the state. Gwen not only credited her previous success as superintendent of schools for appointment to this outstanding school district but also from the very positive endorsements that the district received from superintendent colleagues and state education officials.

Southpointe Heights was a very progressive school district of four thousand students located near a major research university. The school district was consistently rated as one of the top five school districts in the state, if not number one, based on students performing extremely well on national standardized tests and high rates of student acceptance into the top colleges and universities in the country. Southpointe Heights was one of the wealthiest school districts in the state, with a community that appreciated and supported the academic programs of their school district.

It was not surprising that Gwen found the faculty and the administration, as well as the parents of the district, to be very proud of the historical achievements of their children and optimism about their future. They were all united in their quest to continue their fine tradition of educational excellence, as well as very insistent on being involved in school district decision-making and strategic planning. Gwen was elated to be named superintendent of such a high performing, prestigious, and wealthy school district that rewarded her handsomely for her curriculum expertise and instructional leadership.

However, the parents of Southpointe Heights were often referred to as "Gold Medallion Helicopter Parents" of the region by the area media. The faculty was referred to as "Intellectual Trendsetters" by the same media. But Gwen soon discovered that both of these groups wanted "to be in charge" of directing any change to their traditional view of their programs and curriculum. The teachers wanted their superintendent to send a strong message to parents "to stay out of their buildings" until invited by the administration, while the parents wanted Gwen to "keep the teachers in their place, since we pay their salaries and they are our public servants!"

By the end of the first year, Gwen had compiled a 360-degree strategic analysis of the school district that resulted in her personal ranking of the key cultural traits of the school district including the following reflective appraisals:

- There is a talented group of central- and building-level administrators at Southpointe Heights whose egotistical attitudes often created more problems than they solved.
- The parents of Southpointe Heights are supportive, difficult, feel entitled because of their status in the region and their high tax rates, and demand excellence in curriculum and instruction.
- The high-quality teachers are often difficult, feel entitled because of their instructional outcomes and high salaries in the region, and are professionally demanding as well.
- The community has a solid and long history of providing considerable amounts of financial and material resources to the school district. School district budgets are routinely supported without much rancor and dissent.
- The board of education has, more times than not, supported the parents over the faculty especially as related to curriculum and instruction choices, opportunities, and student placements.
- All stakeholders have recently felt a strong frustration at the increasing amount of interference from the state in terms of mandates, testing, and standardization that has led many in the community to recently advocate for "non-compliance" to statewide initiatives since, in their not-so-humble opinion, those changes were designed to improve other districts in the state so they could eventually rise to the educational excellence level of Southpointe Heights.
- A "Competing, Aggressive, Challenging, and Entitled Culture" was evident throughout the Southpointe Heights Central School District.

At the start of her second year as superintendent, Gwen was faced with a new state mandate that school districts implement a state-endorsed standardized testing program for all students in grades two through twelve. Gwen knew that the members of the board of education and the community would not be happy with this directive that superimposed testing requirements that were significantly below the standards already in place within the Southpointe School System.

The parents and most of the faculty felt that their tests and measurements for student achievement were far more demanding than the new mandated state testing program and much more individually based as they were pioneers in using student portfolios and multiple measures of grade level proficiency. Simply put, most Southpointe stakeholders agreed that their local tests and assessments were far superior to anything produced by the company contracted by the state.

Parents also felt that the state assessment program was too restrictive and structured. They believed that the state testing program forced their teachers to "teach to the test" and thus diminished the value placed on their historically superior learning opportunities for Southpointe students including numerous exploratory field trips, student performances, and international exchanges that enhanced and individualized the curriculum for their children.

The Southpointe Parent Teachers Association (PTA) demanded that the board of education pass a resolution in opposition to this new state mandated testing program and also encourage all parents to not allow any of their children to be tested in this "archaic and pedestrian" fashion. They contended and empirically evidenced that their local enhanced curriculum and assessment programs resulted in greater demonstrated learning experiences and were highly regarded as a key achievement benchmark by the best colleges and universities for the past seventy-five years!

After considerable dialogue and several open meetings on the subject, the board of education unanimously passed the PTA-generated resolution upon a rather weak recommendation from the superintendent. They also directed Superintendent Osterberg to lobby "her friends" at the state education department for a variance that would allow Southpointe to continue to test and measure the achievement of their students as they have historically and successfully done.

Their commitment was to Southpointe students and not to comply with the state mandate that was part of a federal government program that related to additional funding being channeled to the state for their redistribution to school districts. And given the economic status of Southpointe, they would not realize much positive financial impact anyway. The board strongly advocated their "local control" right over education.

Shortly after this decision by the Southpointe Board of Education, four other nearby school districts that also felt their curriculum and assessment programs were superior to those being imposed by the state offered to join Southpointe Heights in their "fight for local control" of their educational programs. Various community, faculty, and administrative groups and organizations circulated similar petitions in the region to inform the state education officials that several school districts and stakeholders did not appreciate this convergence approach in curriculum and testing and the apparent loss of local control of the quality programs based on local context expectations.

Some of the more experienced and well-respected administrators and teachers in the region provided the following "Animal School" (Reavis, 1937) historical reading as a reference metaphor to rally and sustain support for the petitions against statewide control and compliance to policies focused on standards-based convergence:

> Once upon a time, the animals decided they must do something heroic
> to meet the problems of a new world. So they organized a school.

They adopted an activity curriculum consisting of running, climbing, swimming and flying. To make it easier to administer the curriculum, all the animals took all the subjects.

The duck was excellent in swimming, in fact better than his instructor, but he made only passing grades in flying and was very poor in running. Since he was slow in running, he had to stay after school and also drop swimming in order to practice running. This was kept up until his webbed feet were badly worn and he was only average in swimming. But average was acceptable in school, so nobody worried about that except the duck.

The rabbit started at the top of the class in running, but had a nervous breakdown because of so much make-up work in swimming.

The squirrel was excellent in climbing until he developed frustration in the flying class where his teacher made him start from the ground up instead of from the treetop down. He also developed "Charlie horses" from over-exertion and then got a "C" in climbing and a "D" in running.

The eagle was a problem child and was disciplined severely. In the climbing class he beat all the others to the top of the tree but insisted on using his own way of getting there.

At the end of the year, an abnormal eel that could swim exceedingly well, and also run, climb, and fly a little had the highest average and was valedictorian.

The prairie dogs stayed out of school and fought the tax levy because administration would not add digging and burrowing to the curriculum. They apprenticed their child to a badger and later joined the ground hogs and gophers to start a successful private school.

Some astute individuals even reminded Superintendent Osterberg that she had in fact distributed it to the faculty at the opening of school ceremony two years earlier! However, the request to the state for a variance from the state testing mandate drew an unexpectedly harsh response from the state education department officials. The state informed the superintendent that if the school district continued to process this variance request they were jeopardizing their state aid and she could be considered insubordinate.

When the school board was so informed, it agreed to move forward with their request in spite of the threats from the state. However, the resolve to continue the protest to the state by some of the other school districts and their respective superintendents in the region was reduced and in most cases eliminated by these state education department threats.

And Gwen Osterberg was also specifically reminded by her friends at the state education department to "not take this rebuke of the variance request as anything personal as this was now the way the state was doing education business so it could comply with the federal aid mandates."

That statement alone sent "shivers down Gwen's back" as it conjured up strong negative thoughts! But this also reminded her that she is, in fact, an "agent of the state" and is, therefore, obligated to enforce all the "laws, regulations, and mandates" of the state education department as part of her duties. If she did not comply, her certification to practice as a superintendent may be revoked for the "willful neglect of assignments and responsibilities."

Gwen was now truly wrestling on the horns of a major dilemma. She could cognitively and emotionally comprehend the state's need for compliance to this new testing mandate as she personally knew and experienced some educational accountability problems in her previous school districts and she was, after all, licensed and entrusted to promulgate the regulations and mandates of the state education department. But the board of education and community were her "employers" and they strongly demanded that she champion for their "local control rights."

In addition, her cardinal educational values were congruent with curriculum divergence and the individualization of instruction and not curriculum convergence and standardization.

Gwen struggled about how to best resolve this dilemma of compliance versus commitment. She knew that her decision should be consistent with her values and long-standing administrative mantra, to always "make decisions based on doing what is in the best interest of students." But she also respected the regulations and mandates of the state education department that she had a professional obligation to uphold and promote.

And she was also pressured by some of her state education department friends and other superintendents who privately admonished her, "don't do anything aggressively that may jeopardize your professional standing and your career potentials."

Gwen knew what she should do, but was questioning if it was the best thing to do, given the context of the situation. How could she not be consistent with her core values and the demands of constituents, yet how could she not support the mandates of the state education department in their pursuit to raise student achievement and obtain additional federal funding?

And what about the professional costs to her related to her thoughts about the testing mandates: Was she tarnishing her reputation as a student-centered educator or was she influencing her future in a negative way to do more good for more students as a recognized educational leader?

Gwen Osterberg's dilemma caused her many sleepless nights and much stress and anxiety as she weighed her options and approaches related to this issue: Should she advocate for compliance or should she advocate for commitment?

In the popular sitcom *Seinfeld*, one episode describes a soup restaurant run by Yev, who is temperamental, regimental, and rigid, especially in the ordering procedure for his popular soup. In his store, if you want his soup, then you must comply with his established procedures. Failure to comply with these procedures results in "no soup for you," as Jerry's friend Elaine finds out when she refuses to meticulously comply with Yev's pre-set rules for queuing, ordering, and paying at his establishment.

During these times of increased accountability and funding tied to performance, superintendents across the nation are faced with the dilemma of how to motivate staff to not only reach mandated goals, but exceed them as well. A critical component of school superintendent leadership is to find the balance between compliance with external mandates and commitment from those implementing the mandate.

To comply or "no soup [state and/or federal funds] for you" analogy is a key dilemma for school superintendents. However, a deeper examination suggests that superintendents may be faced with the dilemma of commitment versus compliance within the educational community.

Considering the current environment of standards-driven convergence and focused accountability, it can become challenging for superintendents to authentically motivate the educational community in the quest to reach externally set standardized goals. Given the bureaucratic nature and hierarchical chain of command that exists in state education systems, the dynamic that exists between compliance and commitment may be strained.

It is the leader's responsibility to frame the context of the decisions that need to be made regarding the quest to achieve standardized goals. Establishing and sustaining goals in public education is a complex process that requires ongoing engagement by those leading change. A school district may best be served by using a coordinated centralized/decentralized framework that is situation specific.

Without reasonable coordination, it may not be possible to create compliance alignment; without decentralization it will not be possible to facilitate the sharing of information about emerging student learning needs to gain personal commitment.

Leadership is both simple and complex. At its core, leadership provides direction and exercises influence through desirable effective communication. How well leaders interact within the larger social and organizational context will determine success. As mentioned in ELLC Standard 6 educational leaders "promote the success of all students by not only understanding but responding to, and influencing the larger political, social, economic, legal, and cultural context." The leader balances the rigidity and flexibility as necessary. Likewise, policy makers need to be aware of this balance between rigidity and flexibility.

A word of caution: manipulation may be necessary. While one may find the word "manipulation" to imply control and rigidity, sometimes it may be inevitable to frame a decision process in this manner. Once framed, then collaborative leadership can be put into effect; but throughout the process, using input from followers should be encouraged and reflected upon. The leader may need to alter decision-making and problem-solving approaches to fit the context.

A major responsibility of the school superintendent is to create a culture within the school system that supports a total commitment to continuous improvement regardless of previous student achievement. The superintendent's approach should begin with a strategy that establishes clear goals and a framework for continuously evaluating instructional programs, teaching methods, and valid testing procedures. Appropriate goal setting can be motivating as well as ensuring educational community commitment.

If we want to provide our children with an opportunity to compete effectively in tomorrow's economy, we must transform our schools into world-class educational institutions. Superintendents cannot run from state directive compliance issues that advocate student growth and teacher accountability. Rather, they can treat the mandate as an opportunity — an opportunity to continue to build and lead a transformed educational system that is based on critical reflective practice and policy debate.

VOICES FROM THE ARENA

Scholars

- "Moral purpose is about both ends and means. In education, an important end is to make a difference in the lives of students." (Michael Fullan)
- "The key to all this is involving team members on establishing norms, and then holding everyone accountable to what they agreed upon." (Patrick Lencioni)
- "Change threatens our self-esteem. New conditions require of us fresh skills, abilities and attitudes but we lack the confidence that we are up to the new challenges." (James O'Toole)
- "So for many organizations, faced with renewal, salvation can only come from the outside." (John Gardner)
- "If people do not want to put in the additional work required without some evidence that the situation will improve . . . there will be resistance." (Rosabeth Kanter)
- "Our greatest glory is in never falling, but in rising every time we fall." (Confucius)
- "My life is my message." (Mahatma Gandhi)
- "But not to acknowledge a mistake, not to correct it and learn from it, is a mistake of a different order. It usually puts a person on a self-deceiving, self-justifying path, often involving rationalization to self and to others." (Stephen Covey)

- "The more people are committed the less need for a mechanism to control their behavior." (Amitai Etzioni)

Practicing Superintendents

- "I have a strong belief in educating kids . . . anything that deters or undermines the process . . . I will take a stand . . . it is that simple." (Rural school superintendent)
- "One must possess a well-established philosophy. You need to spend time reflecting and continuing to work hard on its implementation." (Suburban school superintendent)
- "It took two years to develop a mission and vision statement. No need for staff to be able to recite it but at least to wear it on their sleeves. There should be a commitment to the statements. Programs that reflect these statements will likely follow." (Rural school superintendent)
- "You must be able to recognize self-serving issues . . . yours as well as others." (Rural school superintendent)
- "It is not about you. On important issues you need to get opinions from your staff." (Suburban school superintendent)
- "It is all about responsibility. You can delegate but you cannot delegate responsibility. When you empower others be sure they have the right skills to do the job." (Rural school superintendent)
- "I was able to build strong relationships. Strong beliefs of what public education is all about." (Suburban school superintendent)

REFLECTION

1. Is the development of a shared vision the outcome of change; is this enough to determine success?
2. How can I as a school leader change the mindsets of some staff members and gain their commitment that all students can learn?
3. While I understand the importance of developing goals, can we be comfortable with never fully arriving since there is no end date to education?
4. What conditions need to be present in our schools to effect powerful change for obtaining long-term commitment?

FIVE

Problems vs. Predicaments

If I had an hour to solve a problem and my life depended on the solution, I would spend the first 55 minutes determining the proper question to ask, for once I know the proper question; I could solve the problem in less than five minutes.
— Albert Einstein

Life is not a spectacle or feast: it's a predicament.
— George Santayana

We submit that most of us—whether in leadership roles or followership roles—prefer to think that life and dealing with its many peaks and valleys is pretty linear and rational (notwithstanding irrational people). When faced with a problem or a decision to be made, we like to identify the problem, list options, and choose the option that we believe best fits the situation.

Whether we have been formally trained or learned through life's experiences, using a step-by-step approach offers a framework for each of us to hold onto, especially during difficult times. This linear-rational decision-making approach is best described as a combination of both the classical approach and the incremental approach articulated by Hoy and Miskel (2008):

- *Classical* approach is the rational systematic means-ends analysis focused on optimizing organizational goals.
- *Incremental* approach is the successive search for reasonable alternatives to facilitate good decision-making.

Superintendents are no different. Faced with daily crises, criticism from every direction, and trying to balance their personal life with their public life, the linear-rational approach provides something to hold onto as various school administration issues are identified and brought for-

53

ward to be resolved. However, as we listen and observe superintendents, it becomes more and more evident that leading a school district in the contemporary context is anything but linear and rational. A number of superintendents implied that using the linear-rational approach is much like sticking a thumb in a leaking dike—thinking the problem has been solved—when another leak appears.

But superintendent training has, for the most part, emphasized this linear-rational approach to problem solving and decision-making; yet when this approach is used over and over again and the results are less than optimum, there is a tendency to keep using this approach, in spite of the lack of success. As a result, the linear-rational approach (this is how to do it) is very appealing, much like a life preserver for a struggling swimmer.

Superintendents are often asked (or told) to solve very complex problems, make difficult decisions, and make sure that everyone supports them. However, it is when this approach does not work that superintendents become upset, frustrated, defensive, and aggressive—yet they generally still keep going back to the linear-rational approach because that is their most common decision-making paradigm.

Why would they keep going back to something that does not work? One issue we discovered is that training modules, best practices, and the "new way to lead" all provide a framework for the linear-rational approach paradigm. We have seen management change to leadership, environment to culture, resources to assets and back, weaknesses to challenges, MBO to TQM (management by objectives to total quality management), and a million iterations in between. The reoccurring underlining theme to solve problems is, we believe, the linear-rational approach.

The question that needs to be answered is: Does the public that the superintendent serves understand that many contemporary educational problems are really systemic predicaments that are more universal in nature than easily solved at the local level? For example, we know that poverty, parental education, and other social issues affect student learning and achievement. One needs only to check the zip code of a school to know the levels of student achievement.

Yet superintendents are held accountable for student learning (or lack thereof) with factors they have absolutely no control over. These are the type of predicaments superintendents face.

It has been said that problems are issues that have the potential to be solved, while predicaments are situations in which there are no solutions. A problem is created when something goes wrong, a mistake is made, or there is an error in judgment or just an unfortunate incident. A problem calls for a solution and can be managed. A series of steps are taken in which the problem can be identified, options listed, values considered, and a decision can be made in how best to resolve the problem. And the linear-rational paradigm fits best whether based on the classical model, the incremental model, or a combination of both decision-making models.

With a predicament, there are no solutions and the leader tries to make the best of the situation at hand, knowing that one may not be in control of the environment in which the predicament is occurring. We tend to face predicaments with responses such as denial, anger, depression, and, in some cases, acceptance. Whatever the response, however, the predicament is not solved and the solutions appear as exigent bandages to copious systematic hemorrhaging.

For example, if it is raining on your wedding day, and the ceremony and reception were to be outside, you can solve this problem by moving it inside. However, there is really no way to resolve the issue of the weather itself. Canceling the wedding and waiting for the weather to change would not be practical. As a matter of fact, a preferred way of dealing with a predicament might be found in the old adage of "riding out the storm."

There are numerous similar expressions that are popular descriptions of a predicament, such as:

- Between a rock and a hard place.
- In a pickle.
- Damned if you do, damned if you don't.
- No way out.

Another descriptive example of a predicament is found in Joseph Heller's (1961) classic book, *Catch-22*. In one particular telling scene, Doc Daneeka explains why he can't ground either Yossarian or Orr due to insanity:

> There was only one catch and that was Catch-22, which specified that a concern for one's own safety in the face of dangers that were real and immediate was the process of a rational mind. Orr was crazy and could be grounded. All he had to do was ask; and as soon as he did, he would no longer be crazy and would have to fly more missions.
> Orr would be crazy to fly more missions and sane if he didn't, but if he was sane he had to fly them. If he flew them he was crazy and didn't have to; but if he didn't want to he was sane and had to. Yossarian was moved very deeply by the absolute simplicity of this clause of Catch-22 and let out a respectful whistle.
> "That's some catch, that catch-22," he observed. "It's the best there is," Doc Daneeka agreed.

Superintendents are living on the horns of similar dilemmas everyday as they provide leadership and resolve issues related to their students, faculty, and community. Some key contemporary educational issues are predicaments more than they are problems and like the *Catch-22* dilemma present the leader with choices that, although logical and viable, cannot truly address and solve the issues. This type of dilemma causes much leadership consternation and frustration and often times results in the leader simply giving up (and seeking other leadership positions) or giving in to the prevailing organizational perceptions that the issue is an enigma beyond leadership control.

Some leaders directly attempt to address these issues and, subsequently, face the political realities that their probing into the predicament too frequently and with too much verve may result in their demise as the organizational leader at that time. Other superintendents have identified that these predicaments are best addressed when they are closer to retirement and, thus, the personal cost to them is not as great as it was earlier in their careers. Still others bear the burden and feel the personal and professional pain of living on the horns of the problems versus predicaments dilemma and experience great stress due to their inability to solve the issues within their leadership purview.

SUPERINTENDENT'S STORY: BETWEEN A ROCK AND A HARD PLACE

After a review of the expectations of the advertised position for superintendent, Jason Crick decided to apply for the superintendency of the East River City School District. He knew it was a long shot but thought, "why not?" His three children were now in college or had graduated from college. His wife strongly supported his decision. She thought that the position would not only be professionally rewarding but that it may be exciting living in a large city.

In every leadership position Jason held, he was successful. He felt that his current position as superintendent in a small-city school district certainly provided him with an excellent background for assuming a large-city school district superintendency. After all, it only meant adding a few zeros to student enrollment, staffing, facilities, and the budget. The job was basically the same. The board was the same in size with each having nine members but there was still a lingering feeling on the large-city board that they represented geographically a certain section of the city.

Jason felt comfortable addressing large groups of people. The media attention in the small-city district was not overwhelming, so he thought he could handle the increased interest in a large-city environment. He knew he was articulate and he viewed the increased emphasis on quality schools as an opportunity. With all of this he felt in control.

Even though the board hired a consultant with national ties, the process for hiring followed an expected process. There would be the placement of ads, screen applicants, focus groups would meet with the consultant, interviews with community groups, open forums, candidate presentation, tour of the district, and board interview and dinner. The spouse was included in all of the activities. During the board interview process it appeared that one board member was assigned to watch the facial expressions of his wife as Jason responded to questions.

He thought he did extremely well throughout the process and was not surprised when he was selected by the board with a 7–2 vote. His contract was finalized for board approval with negotiations between his attorney and the board's attorney. This step bothered him. He did not feel this was a good way to start a positive relationship. In two previous superintendencies he represented himself.

However, Jason was advised by the State Association of Superintendents that it was in his best interest to have outside representation. He took their advice only to experience later that it was a wise move. The contract was for three years renewable at the end of his second year of service. In addition to his base salary the contract also included health benefits for him and his wife after retirement, a split whole life policy, and a bonus of $50,000 should his contract be renewed after the second year.

Jason insisted that at least two sessions be devoted to his appraisal of performance, and a process be mutually developed that included the following: the setting of priorities, a job description that clearly identifies areas of discretionary responsibilities, setting of standards of expectations, and the procedures for conducting of the evaluation.

During the interview process with the board, Jason emphasized the importance of hitting the ground running. He told the board that he would develop such a plan—an Entry Plan. Along with the Entry Plan he would make use of a procedure called Manage by Walking Around (MBWA). The process is simple but time consuming.

The first step for developing the Entry Plan was to identify internal groups (teachers, custodians, cafeteria staff, etc.) and external groups (parents, government officials, police, etc.) and ask them to participate in an interview consisting of several questions. Typical questions included: What are the major strengths of this district? What are the areas in need of greatest improvement? In what three areas would you want to place the major focus for district improvement over the next three years? The Management by Wandering Around was used to validate the Entry Plan results.

The process began with an observation tour of the district keeping in mind what was reported in the Entry Plan. The board strongly supported this approach. He felt that he was in control and taking the beginning steps for hitting the ground running.

In his report to the board Jason identified many problems. After further analysis several resembled predicaments—situations that were beyond his control using the linear-rational problem-solving paradigm. The list of problems from those most often mentioned to those least often mentioned was as follows:

- The achievement gap between students based on social economic status (SES) was becoming wider and wider each year.
- Large numbers of students did not have the same opportunity to receive a quality instructional program because of the configuration of the high school programs based on attendance areas.
- Student attendance was at an all-time low. Graduation rates were reported to be the lowest in the state.
- Agreement to receive needed state funding was dependent on a teacher evaluation process that required union and district approval. Two clauses held up the agreement: that at least 20 percent of the evaluation processes contain student achievement results as measured by the state's paper and pencil standardized tests and that the teacher is held partially accountable for student attendance.
- District Parent Coordinating Councils are urging families to transfer their children out of struggling schools to those schools that are achieving better results.
- The adults of the school communities are rarely involved in the education of their children.
- State aid has been reduced while charter schools are on the increase based on statewide policies.
- Schools no longer represent diversity, in fact, there has been a re-segregation based on school choice factors such as: academic vs. vocational, arts and humanities vs. athletics, liberal education vs. school to work transitions.
- Failure to begin "turn around plans" for two high schools by an outside consulting group.
- School board membership was becoming less desirable.
- The most alarming comments were by teachers, administrators, and some parents who reported or observed the following:
  - A father comes into the administrative office, yells at his son (the student), and starts to beat the child with a belt.
  - A student was caught smoking marijuana in the bathroom and when the parent came to school yelled "that bastard, that's where my weed's been going."
  - During a parent/teacher conference a parent proclaimed that the son needed to stay away from street life because "he is not as much of a shark as is his father."
  - Several families do not have a home so they sleep in their cars in the evening.
  - A teacher was told not to call the parents anymore because they have given up on their child.
  - One parent said do not bother her anymore: "That's your problem." You do not understand "my culture."

- A teacher reported that she made 120 phone calls encouraging parents to attend a school meeting to discuss changes in the curriculum. Four parents were in attendance at the meeting.

In the past Jason knew that he should not internalize "what is" but these comments were extremely stressful. The East River City School District was at a crossroads — and most people did not get it. He wondered where this district and its previous administrations left the "Trolley Tracks?" Why, when, and how are we going to turn things around? He was determined to lead in the best interests of the children of the district in the hopes that this would eventually stabilize things and provide a focus for real school reform.

The district was, indeed, in a crisis mode. He thought that he would need to follow a centralized/directive approach with input from others as opposed to a decentralized approach/distributive leadership approach. However, it was important for him to be able to ask the right questions and authentically be viewed as not always having the right answers. Despite the recognition that the district was in crisis, the board was insisting that all plans be developed focusing on "collaboration." Bold moves without community input and faculty consent were out of the question.

After the board meeting Jason shared his thoughts with his leadership team, which consisted of all central office administrators at the supervisory level. Nearly all agreed that these were the issues of the East River City School District and were the issues for a very long period of time. What disappointed him most was that few were ready to offer possible solutions. They all seemed to accept the predicaments as immutable and part and parcel of the "way it is" in East River City.

However, Jason believed in himself and in miracles; the district was in crisis and he knew he had to hit a "Roy Hobbs" home run to turn things around. He knew he should not swing at every pitch, or worse yet swing before the ball was pitched. He was willing to accept the heat. He was up to the challenge and felt energized to directly and honestly attack the predicaments of education in this city school district.

After six months his appointment appeared more and more like "Mission Impossible." A "Roy Hobbs" home run was never hit in spite of his increased focused efforts to be highly visible in the community and enthusiastically portray his visions for improved education for all children. The media was somewhat supportive largely due to monthly meetings with the editorial board of the newspaper. However, feedback from board members, staff, community leaders, and parents only increased tension regarding his preferred plan to turn things around.

In spite of some progress on test scores, school attendance, and parental relationships, progress was not at the level expected. It was becoming increasingly difficult to navigate on a daily basis the constraints of relationships with people, personalities, contracts, and political pressures. He was experiencing an educational leadership "Catch-22." If he directly addressed the predicaments, he was judged to be too idealistic, and if he chose not to address some of those previously identified predicaments, he was judged to be too uncaring.

There were now personal attacks on him as a school district leader. A vote of "no confidence" by the teachers' union personally hurt because he thought relationships were good since he was able to work with them on several issues that were not resolved by the previous superintendents. This union stance appeared to be heading toward a relationship that would only exist if attention was devoted to a "what have you done for us today?" mentality. In spite of the union position he felt that he could work with their executive board in promoting improved teaching and learning practices, if he only had more time to do so.

To make matters worse, school board elections were held and the character of the board dramatically changed with the election of three new board members. The dynamics were now radically different from the board that hired him. On many sensitive issues "block voting" became the preferred approach. On personnel appointments, often the process resembled "a friends and family plan"—to him it appeared that the board members were more self-interested as evidenced by their recent hirings than they were interested in improving education for all children of the district.

Jason had instituted a shared-decision-making hiring model and it seemed to be reinforcing a patronage approach more than it was improving the quality of the faculty and staff based on the needs of students.

He also reorganized central office to make the organization "flatter" and more responsive to the needs of the building principals. Many believed that the process of reorganization was fair and transparent and that it was important to have the right people in the right positions to make sure the right things were done for children.

However, what began to surface in his mind was the thought that this city school district may not be governable. It was more than a problem: it was a governance predicament based on context history and years of self-ingratiating unions and school community groups.

The first step in the process necessitated that he begin to recognize whether or not he was dealing with a problem or a predicament. A predicament required a different mindset by expanding thinking beyond what existed in the schools. Jason felt strongly that he had reasonable control over processes that encouraged collaboration in and outside the four walls of the school environment but the results of these efforts often led to a lack of commitment. Awareness on the part of the building administration, faculty, and school communities was controllable but implementation of changes to address the large-scale predicaments of the district was a different story.

Jason knew that change would be slow and non-sequential. It would not be linear and rational at all times. He often told his administrators and lead teachers, "We'll go as fast as we can to change the East River School District and as slow as we must to assure that we are doing the right changes for the benefit of our children." No question there was a need for urgency but within a sustainable time commitment. In spite of the lack of total commitment by the teachers' union, he still felt there were issues where collaboration was possible.

The issue of teacher evaluation based partly on student achievement and attendance seemed to be a good place to start. Jason was silently in agreement that this aspect could be improved if the process took into consideration student socio-economic status, language background, student mobility, class size, and teacher experience; then it would be a fairer measure of teacher performance. He strongly supported the teachers on this issue.

More importantly, he felt as they did, that we are witnessing a real crisis in education that by forcing teachers to teach to the test we are de-professionalizing the profession and forcing convergence in the curriculum at the expense of creativity and the joy of learning. On one horn of this dilemma there is the problem of the implementation of a standardized teacher evaluation program for accountability's sake, and on the other horn we have the predicament of meeting the developmentally appropriate needs of students in creative learning environments.

However, Jason confronted other pieces of this contemporary city school organizational puzzle besides teacher evaluation that on the surface appear to be controllable such as: his own evaluation, the insistence that the district be aligned in all schools for promoting student achievement, collaboration with all those who have an interest, and the ability to provide high-quality data that link to student achievement.

A different path was needed that required patience and time as well as bold leadership strokes but he began to realize that the public he served was not forgiving of the various decisions that were made to put the district "back on track," especially those that tore at the historical and political fabric of their city. Soon there were signals that the public for whom he worked so hard and tirelessly was beginning to clamor for new school leadership.

Or perhaps they desired a different kind of leadership, one that would move slower and more methodically, dare we say, in a more linear and rational manner and one that would address more problems but less predicaments.

Jason continued to question his leadership ability to survive such a diametrically opposed challenge to his leadership approach. He reflected about his ability to truly convince this public that short term results be viewed as necessary before a process of institutionalization could be achieved.

He also wondered if it is possible for him or anyone else to successful-ly lead a city school district representing diverse cultures coupled with a multitude of interest groups with different visions of quality. Surely this school district resonated with predicaments that needed limited but long-term solutions and he, truly, was living on the horns of this dilemma at East River City School District.

According to the research recently conducted by the authors, superin-tendents in their first few years in the position may attempt to address predicaments believing they are problems to be solved. However, once they become immersed in these problems that are really unsolvable pre-dicaments and they experience the political whiplash from their various constituencies, they tend to back off from these issues and pursue other more solvable problems of their school district.

However, our study also revealed that those experienced and effective superintendents who feel the "safety net" of the twilight of their respec-tive careers, believe that it is appropriate and necessary for them to fol-low the Don Quixote route and pursue solving predicaments. Subse-quently, it is imperative for new and aspiring superintendents to recog-nize the difference between problems and predicaments as exemplified in this chapter.

Superintendents and those who prepare them should keep in mind the following admonition from Reinhold Niebuhr (1932): "God grant me the serenity to accept the things I cannot change; courage to change the things I can; and wisdom to know the difference."

FROM THE ARENA

Scholars

- "Sometimes people resist change because of personal concerns about their ability to be effective after the change. Can I do it? All of a sudden the change demands a new set of competencies." (Rosab-eth Kanter)
- "This is why close relationships are not ends in themselves. Collab-orative cultures, which by definition have close relationships, are indeed powerful, but unless they are focusing on the right things may end up powerfully wrong." (Michael Fullan)
- "If we want to lead efforts to improve the way things are, we must be willing to take risks." (James Kouzes and Barry Posner)
- "Enable potential leaders to escape the bondage of 'what is' and point the way toward what might be." (John Gardner)
- "Change requires that the powerful admit they have been wrong." (James O'Toole)

- "Often we are puzzled by the causes of our problems; when we merely need to look at our own solutions to other problems in the past." (Peter Senge)
- "It is tempting, if the only tool you have is a hammer, to treat everything as if it were a nail." (Abraham Maslow)
- "At last, he began to think as you or I would have thought at first; for it is always the person not in the predicament who knows what ought to have been done in it, and would unquestionably have done it too." (Charles Dickens)

Practicing Superintendents

- "The job is not about having the right answers all the time, but asking the right questions." (Rural school superintendent)
- "Park your ego at the door." (Rural school superintendent)
- "You must be able to sort out the implications of a decision. Who else might be affected?" (Suburban school superintendent)
- "We need to get away from relying on demographics and do the job. Too often demographics are used as an excuse for poor student achievement." (Small-city school superintendent)
- "We need to be honest with respect to our performance and the performance of others on staff." (Small-city school superintendent)
- "We are at a crossroads in education. People do not just get it. There are some large-scale problems in education that are simply not solvable in a short period of time." (Small-city school superintendent)

REFLECTION

1. What conditions need to be present to effect powerful/sustainable change in a school system embedded with predicaments?
2. Is it possible to create an environment that is conducive to change where anxiety and tension exist because of multiple diverse interest groups?
3. Should student test scores be a part of teacher evaluation? Student attendance?
4. What resources or strategies can we incorporate to create a common vision for school improvement and student well-being?
5. Has the emphasis on state assessment testing had a negative or positive effect on public education? On teaching and learning?

SIX
Leadership vs. Management

Managers are people who do things right and leaders are people who do the right thing.
The manager administers; the leader innovates.
The manager maintains; the leader develops.
The manager relies on control; the leader inspires trust.
The manager focuses on systems and structures; the leader focuses on people.
— Warren Bennis

Imagine, for a moment, there are two equally and supremely talented basketball teams. Team A has a coach who is motivational, inspiring, collaborative, and a model for all things good about molding a successful team. Strategies, proper conditioning, teamwork, and a vision for success are but a few of the leadership behaviors the coach uses to influence the team — individually, as well as collectively.

Philosophically, the coach believes that the best way to prepare his team is to learn several fundamental approaches to the game. The coach, who is as competitive as any coach, knows that winning is important but feels just as strongly that nurturing relationships and getting the team to improve "one day at a time — one game at a time" are equally important.

Team B, on the other hand, has a coach who recognizes the talents and gifts of his players and, basically, provides a formal framework for the members to play within. The coach has the team practice some very basic fundamentals on a regular basis and prepares for each opponent the same way: "practicing and doing what we do best — keeping things very simple, making sure we do a few things really well." The coach calls the plays and strategies from the bench, and there is little opportunity for the players to "freelance."

Like the first coach, he is a fiery competitor, yet according to this coach, "winning games is why we are here . . . from the first practice to the end of the last game, our goal is to win *every* game and the championship—nothing more, nothing less!"

Now, suppose both teams end up undefeated and win their respective conference championships. Is one team better than the other? Has one coach done a better job of coaching? Which is the best way to coach a team? Does it matter if these are high school teams? College teams? Professional teams?

Scholars have struggled for many decades to answer the question of whether an organization—a team, a company, or a school district—needs a leader or a manager to be successful. Or maybe a little bit of both!

In many ways, leadership and management are similar. To successfully lead an organization, one must have influence with the followers. The same is true for a manager. Collaboration—being able to work together—is necessary for both a leader and a manager. Meeting objectives and reaching goals are also critical components of both leadership and management. Thus, a question that needs to be considered is: What is the difference between leadership and management?

One could argue that management became a critical component of organizational theory during the rise of the industrial revolution in America and elsewhere around the beginning of the twentieth century. For organizations to be effective and efficient, a manager had to be concerned with planning, controlling, coordinating, optimizing, directing, and deciding.

In other words, the manager was placed in a position of authority to provide order, stability, and consistency, while simultaneously ensuring that goals were met, structures were in place, problems solved systematically, and so forth. And with this often came an organizational structure that was very much hierarchical and authoritarian, with the manager in a position of authority.

It is not to say, however, that leadership is not interested in order, stability, consistency, goals, and problem solving. Whereas managers may be viewed as more linear and rational but less relational, leadership can be viewed more as influencing, modeling, inspiring, challenging, engaging, visioning, and transforming the followers to move themselves, as well as the organization, to places they have never been before. One needs to look no further than the current literature available regarding contemporary leadership, which strongly implies that leadership is much more effective than management in creating lasting success.

In the current world of public education in America, boards of education, among others, struggle with the question of whether it is better to have a leader or a manager for their superintendent.

One need only look at advertisements of school superintendent vacancies to get a very strong impression that school boards (and the communities they represent) are sending mixed messages regarding leadership and management when searching for a new superintendent to lead their district. Consider the following samples of such:

> The _____ Board of Education seeks a visionary leader who is willing to advocate for the district and its student body. The new superintendent will build on several successful improvement initiatives and lead the district to higher levels of student achievement. Strong emphasis will be placed on the candidate's ability to work closely with a variety of constituency groups, become a visible force within the community, work in a collaborative fashion, and maintain an unwavering focus on the needs of students.

> The _____ Central School District is seeking an educational leader with a record of administrative accomplishments. The successful candidate will be one who possesses:

- A proven track record of raising achievement for all students.
- A dynamic leadership style that instills confidence in all constituencies.
- Strong interpersonal skills along with the ability to communicate in a clear and concise manner.
- Integrity, energy, and strong desire to promote partnerships within the community.
- The ability to think and plan strategically.

> The _____ School District is seeking the following qualities for its next superintendent:

- Be a strong leader with the ability to interact effectively with all staff members.
- Demonstrate a sincere interest in the education of all students.
- Be skilled in motivating and evaluating staff.
- Be knowledgeable on educational trends.
- Have a record of fiscal responsibility.
- Have the ability to establish a culture of professional and academic excellence.

After a review of the advertisements, one sees that in these instances, the board (school district) is seeking a leader first and a manager second. As a matter of fact, there is more than three times the number of leadership-related qualities mentioned than managerial-related qualities. This is not surprising, considering the emphasis on leadership over management throughout research, preparation programs, and professional development in support of aspiring and sitting superintendents.

However, the question that becomes part of the dilemma is: Do boards of education (school districts) *really* want a superintendent who is a leader in the sense of visioning, inspiring, change-agent, motivator, et cetera?

Or do boards want someone to lead the district who is a more decisive, authoritative, bottom-line type of superintendent?

School superintendents today are very much aware of the need to reassess priorities and the reallocation of resources in order to continue to build a better educational system. Virtually everyone feels that something has gone wrong with education. Liberals accuse the schools of failing to meet the needs of those students who are challenged socially, economically, and/or culturally to the mainstream.

Conservatives charge the schools with waste, extravagance, and even "dumbing down" of curriculum and instruction. Even those in the middle, who generally regard the schools as relatively good, are becoming increasingly concerned about the quality of our schools today and the direction they fear they are heading.

This widespread disillusionment with education has generated intense and sometimes desperate efforts at reform. Throughout the country educators are experiencing these pressures because of a sustained, diverse, and persistent challenge to their ability to lead *and* manage school districts. One need only look back at the past several decades in which educators were presented with A Nation at Risk, Goals 2000, No Child Left Behind, Race to the Top, and most recently, Common Core.

One could argue that each of these initiatives—because of the hierarchical system put into place to implement each—has taken much of the superintendent's (and school principal's) ability to lead away in place of becoming an effective manager, whose primary responsibility is to improve student achievement (read: raise test scores), relying more on management techniques than on leadership.

The irony here is that, for years, critics of public education have strongly suggested that schools adopt a "business model" for success, while corporate America, at least those companies who are considered highly successful, have turned to more "leadership" and "less management" for its chief executives.

This is not to suggest that success is an either/or proposition: leadership or management. One need only review the National Standards for Educational Leaders (CCSSO, 2008) to see the evidence that suggests leadership and management are both critical. While leadership certainly is mentioned and emphasized more, Standard 3 is exclusively dedicated to managerial tasks of school leadership.

As the Wallace Foundation (2013) states,

> Public education's changed mission dictates the need for a new type of leader—an executive instead of an administrator. No longer are school leaders just maintaining the status quo by managing complex operations but like colleagues in business, they must be able to create schools as organizations that can learn and change quickly if they are to improve performance.

Perhaps it is situational. In order to be successful, superintendents need to consider what kind of relationship exists between the leader and followers, the type of tasks that need to be accomplished, and how much support and guidance will be necessary.

While this may be a simplistic approach in deciding to be the leader or manager, the dilemma arises when the superintendent decides to move in one direction and others (e.g., board of education, community, unions) decide that another direction would be more appropriate. Or even worse, if a superintendent is *told* by the board to go in a direction that he or she is not comfortable with or feels is not the wisest direction to take. So the superintendent is caught in yet another dilemma, as the following story depicts.

SUPERINTENDENT'S STORY: LEAD, MANAGE, OR GET OUT OF THE WAY

Richard Green was an assistant superintendent for a large suburban school district located adjacent to a large metropolitan area. He had just completed a doctoral degree program and appeared to be a likely candidate to assume the position of superintendent in his current school district. Dr. Alton Little had been the superintendent for over two decades and was planning to retire at the end of the current school year. During Dr. Little's tenure, the school district had never lost a community budget or capital project vote. Other superintendents jokingly referred to the school district as "Alton's Parish."

However, Richard did not receive the appointment, even though many people connected to the school district thought that he was the heir apparent. By a 6–3 vote, the board decided to offer the position of superintendent to a resident of the community who left the district to become an assistant superintendent in a nearby suburban school district. Little was said or known as to why Richard was not offered the position.

After several months had passed and Richard unable to overcome his disappointment, he decided that perhaps it was time to seek the position of superintendent in another school district. After all, having the position of assistant superintendent should serve as an excellent experience for assuming the position of superintendent. Within a year of applying to a number of districts and having the help of a consultant, Richard was offered the position of superintendent in a small rural district about thirty miles from his home.

The district where Richard was named superintendent was rural, yet in transition. While many of its residents had ties to agriculture, several new housing developments were beginning to spring up throughout the community. Richard was very excited to be part of a growing and changing school district.

Richard assumed the position of superintendent in July. Much to his surprise he was greeted by three new board members, whom he had never met. Two of the previous board members decided not to run for re-election and the third was defeated in the election. At first it did not appear to change the makeup of the board. However, Richard was later to find that one of the newly elected board members was running on a single issue to seek the dismissal of a math teacher and another employee who had close ties to an ultra-conservative organization.

During his first six months, it became evident that this district had been a well-led and well-managed school district. The administrative staff, including the building principals, was considered exceptional. The teaching staff appeared to be competent, although a number of the teachers were considered to be "radical" union members. However, since school budgets were voted on annually by the public and tied to property taxes, budgets were frequently defeated—at least, the first time each spring.

It also did not take very long for Richard to understand that the board of education—including the three new members—had little or no respect for teachers in general. For the most part, the board considered teachers to be liberal, overpaid, and selfish. Thus, when it came to contract negotiations and personnel decisions, the board played a prominent role. In fact, to balance out the influx of teachers from the "outside," the board would often only hire teachers who had ties to the district.

As for contract negotiations, the board and teachers' union often were at odds and such negotiations usually dragged on for months and months. As far as the board was concerned, "good was good enough" and if they (the teachers) did not like it, they could leave!

Richard also found that there were assigned responsibilities beyond the normal scope of most superintendents. Since the district administrative staff was limited to an assistant superintendent for curriculum and a business director, Richard was involved in everything from budgets to buses, athletics to music, human resources to public relations, and almost everything in between! Understanding that this was a smaller district than he was used to, Richard felt very frustrated that he spent most of his time managing the district and not being able to lead the district during these changing times.

Richard's dilemma was that the conservative, long-time families of the district did not want change. They did not want a new standards-based curriculum, or all of this "new technology" that was sweeping schools across the nation. According to them, "good was good enough!"

On the other side were the newcomers to the district. These families had moved from nearby metropolitan areas to get away from urban/suburban issues of congestion and crime, yet wanted this school district to become much more progressive—even if it was more expensive. To them, spending more money equated to better educations for their children.

It was during the second year of his superintendency that Richard felt he had the perfect opportunity to lead the district in a direction that he felt was necessary, considering the changes in curriculum, instruction, and accountability that were being mandated by both the federal government and state government. The current junior/senior high school was built in 1960, with a capacity of one thousand students. Over the next four decades, several additions had been added to the core building. Yet at the present time, there were more than 1,300 students attending the school in grades seven through twelve.

Richard was also very concerned about student achievement in the secondary school. For the past two decades, achievement results from various state assessments consistently placed the students at about the sixtieth percentile in most subject areas. Richard also recognized that the delivery of the instruction at the junior/senior high school was very teacher-centered and traditional.

So Richard began the daunting process of initiating the conversation of building a new high school and turning the old high school into a middle school. He proposed that the high school be designed to support more student-centered curriculum and instruction with up-to-date technology and professional development for teachers in these areas.

As for the older building, Richard proposed that the district adopt the middle school concept of team teaching, interdisciplinary curriculum, and, as with the high school, a dramatic increase in the use of technology, and enhanced professional development for teachers to support this instructional design.

Richard knew that the board would be initially skeptical, so he began to meet with board members individually to discuss these thoughts and ideas. He also spoke to local community groups, parent groups, and pretty much anyone who wanted to hear from him. During the first few months of this, he was pleasantly surprised by the positive feedback he was receiving, especially from the more conservative and traditional-thinking members of the community.

He became even more enthused about this even when consultants came in to survey the project and came up with an estimated cost. While this cost was certainly higher than any project that had been previously proposed in the district, he was able to offset this by informing the board and community that almost 70 percent of the cost would be paid for by the state education department. The remaining 30 percent would be paid for by the local property owners, but would be bonded over thirty years, with the increase on local taxpayers to be less than $200 per year during this time.

For the next six months, Richard spent much of his time meeting with the board, making community presentations, meeting with school construction consultants, and traveling back and forth to the construction and planning agency of the state education department in the capitol. This was very time consuming and at times tiring, but he felt strongly that this kind of leadership was necessary for this project to move forward.

It was during this time, however, that questions about Richard's leadership—more precisely, his management of the district—began to emerge from various sectors of the community, including the board of education. In the beginning, it wasn't anything of major proportions but a series of incidents had people wondering who, in fact, was "running" the district:

- Several minor accidents involving school buses occurred and there were also two instances in which elementary students were dropped off without any parent pick-up.
- A professional development grant worth $100,000 for the next four years was not handed in on time.
- For the first time in four years, the high school graduation rate declined.
- A series of errors from the business office prevented staff from getting their paychecks on time, and several vendors were not paid in a timely manner.

It was not long before the "word on the street" was that Richard was spending more time trying to get support for this new middle and high school configuration than making sure that the district was being managed appropriately. In each case, Richard took responsibility since he was, in fact, "the leader of the district."

However, privately he was surprised at the amount of attention these incidents were getting, since in his previous district, these types of things happened. He was also incensed that the administrators below him—both at the district office and in the schools—did not stand up to take responsibility.

The tipping point occurred when it was reported that an angry parent was found wandering through an elementary school, looking for the teacher who had "put her hands on my child." The police were called and after a few tense moments, the parent was taken away and no one was harmed.

It was at the next board meeting that the unexpected occurred. More than twenty parents spoke up against the lack of safety in the school district. Members of the teachers' union complained about the paycheck fiasco. Another group of parents complained about the declining test scores for high school students.

When they all went into executive session, the board president pointedly told Richard

Either you start running the district the way it ought to be run or, trust me, a change will be made. You are spending way too much time with your grand construction and instruction plans, while the rest of the district isn't doing what it should be doing—and that is teaching and learning in a safe environment. This middle school-new high school stuff is to be placed on the "back burner." As a matter of fact, we don't care if it is ever brought up again. Your job is to make sure this district runs smoothly. Too many parents and too many teachers are complaining way too much. Now do your job like you were hired!

Some people think that leadership and management are inextricably linked and separating them does not make sense. To be successful, a person in a position of authority must have both leadership skills and managerial skills. For example, a superintendent of schools who wishes to have a new high school built must provide the leadership—vision, inspiration, collaboration, and so forth—to garner support for the project. At the same time, he or she must provide the management—proper resource allocation, budgeting, decision-making, etc.—to ensure that the proposal makes financial and educational sense to those who will approve the venture.

Others may argue that leadership, in fact, is different from management. They suggest that leadership is more about the traits and behaviors the person in authority demonstrates. For example, the superintendent above must have both the charisma and charm of a politician involved in a campaign—at all times! They argue that only a "chosen few" have such abilities to be this type of a leader, and if one does not have these traits and behaviors, chances of success are limited, at the very least.

Furthermore, management is not the same as leadership. Management, they contend, is more about making sense of the chaos in overseeing an organization. The superintendent will need to bring order, stability, consistency, and the "bottom-line" to the process for it to be successful.

We submit that leadership and management are both unique and complementary activities. Both have their own functions, characteristics, and qualities, and both are necessary for success. Hence the dilemma for the school superintendent is: Can I be both an effective leader and manager simultaneously? Or is it impossible to be both and if so, will one suffer at the expense of the other?

Based upon our research in this project, as well as that for others, we submit that school superintendents are more likely to manage than to lead. And it is not entirely their fault. As one superintendent shared,

> They [the board] said they wanted a leader . . . someone who could take the district to places it had never been in terms of student achievement, community engagement and so forth. Yet it didn't take long for me to figure out that what they really wanted me to do was stay in the

office and manage the staff, the budget and decision-making. "Thinking-out-of-the-box" was not encouraged or tolerated.

Even in the cases where we observed effective leadership being demonstrated by the superintendent, it was, for the most part, at the expense of effective management. And not surprisingly, when we found superintendents who were effective managers, leadership suffered. Thus, we contend that effective leadership with weak management is just as bad as effective management with weak leadership. Not everyone can excel at being both a leader and manager. Whether it is learned or "in the genes" (or both), some people have the ability to be effective leaders, and others have the ability to be an effective manager.

Yet we submit that superintendents (and boards of education) should be aiming for a balance between effective leadership and effective management. And that is the challenge for this particular dilemma. One needs to go no further than the National Standards for Educational Leaders (CCSSO, 2008) to observe the emphasis on both leadership and management. The standards state:

> A school administrator is an educational leader who promotes the success of all students by:
>
> 1. facilitating the development, articulation, implementation, and stewardship of a vision of learning that is shared and supported by the school community;
> 2. advocating, nurturing, and sustaining a school culture and instructional program conducive to student learning and staff professional growth;
> 3. ensuring management of the organization, operations, and resources for a safe, efficient, and effective learning organization;
> 4. collaborating with families and communities, responding to diverse community interests and needs, and mobilizing community resources;
> 5. acting with integrity, fairness, and in an ethical manner;
> 6. understanding, responding to, and influencing the larger political, social, economic, legal, and cultural context.

Since these standards, in fact, are *leadership* standards, one would expect to see connections to leadership concepts such as *vision, culture, collaborating, acting,* and *influencing.* Perhaps not as explicit, concepts related to management are found throughout the list, including *implementation, ensuring management of, efficient and effective,* and *mobilizing resources.*

Accordingly, the focus of the superintendent—as both the leader and manager of the district—can be divided into three interrelated activities:

1. Deciding what needs to happen and what project(s) needs to be accomplished.
2. How will this project(s) be completed and by whom?

3. What resources—time, money, people, etc.—will be needed in order to successfully complete the project(s)?

In analyzing each of these tasks, one could surmise that each of these activities needs to be accomplished with *both* leadership and management skills. Regarding the first activity, planning (e.g., strategic planning) is a function of management in that goals need to be set, resources allocated, benchmarks created, and so forth.

Yet leadership is critical here as well, since before the management piece described above can be completed, an analysis of the current status of the school district needs to occur, followed by a vision of what the district can become. In order to accomplish this, the superintendent will have to use the leadership skills of influencing, visioning, collaborating, and so on to ensure support for moving in this direction.

Steps 2 and 3, at first glance, appear to be more managerial than leadership oriented. Both are about organizing structures and people in order to successfully reach this new vision. In addition, as the district moves in this direction, problems will need to be solved, decisions will need to be made, controls will need to be put in place, and results will need to be monitored along the way. Each of these strongly suggests management.

Yet leadership must be evident as well. Take for example the use of people in this project. Using the metaphor of the school district (organization) as a bus (Collins, 2001), does the superintendent have the *right* people on the bus and are they sitting in the *right* seats? If the project is to succeed, the leadership of the superintendent will need to emphasize the communication and collaboration of the vision for this project (who is driving the bus), as so aptly stated in ISLLC Standards 1 and 3, and with what Kouzes and Posner (2007) suggest about what exemplary leadership is: "modeling the way, inspiring a shared vision, challenge the process, enable others to act, encourage the heart."

As the superintendent attempts to move the district in a direction that leads to unprecedented success, ensuring proper alignment of resources will be critical—particularly human resources. From a managerial perspective, the superintendent will need to have a plan including goals, strategies, benchmarks, and so forth. He or she will need to have systems in place to monitor and, if necessary, adjust the plan.

This will, however, require leadership as well, since motivation and inspiration will be necessary to create a sense of urgency, energy, and willingness on the part of everyone to contribute to the process in order for success to occur. The balancing act for the superintendent is classic leadership versus management: inspire and motivate or push and be task oriented.

Management and leadership are different. Specific skill sets and functions define these differences. Both are important and both are needed for organizational success. Superintendents as leaders need to be skilled at both of these. The dilemma occurs when the superintendent is skilled in one and lacking in the other or fails to apply the right process for a given situation. This usually occurs when the superintendent receives mixed messages on which one needs to be emphasized, according to the board and/or the community.

In reality, it should *not* be an either/or proposition. Superintendents can become effective leader-managers. However, it is only when everyone understands the differences between leadership and management, as well as the uniqueness and critical nature of both, that superintendents will be able to provide the appropriate leadership for the district and be able to get out from under the dilemma of "do I lead or do I manage?"

FROM THE ARENA

Scholars

- "The single biggest way to impact an organization is to focus on leadership development. There is almost no limit to the potential of an organization that recruits good people, raises them up as leaders and then continually develops them." (John Maxwell)
- "A leader is someone who makes decisions. Sometimes they turn out right and sometimes they turn out wrong; but either way, decisions are made." (Anonymous)
- "The very essence of leadership is that you have to have a vision. It's got to be a vision you articulate early and often on every occasion. You can't blow a weak trumpet." (Theodore Hesburgh)
- "Actions do speak louder than words. Manuals don't count. Leadership is good work, not simply good talk." (Max DePree)
- "The best leader is the one who has sense enough to pick good men to do what he wants done, and then self-restraint to keep from meddling with them while they do it." (Theodore Roosevelt)
- "The key to successful leadership is influence, not authority." (Ken Blanchard)
- "Underperforming organizations are usually over-managed and under-led." (Warren Bennis)

Practicing Superintendents

- "All they [the board] wanted to talk about during the interview was leadership, leadership, leadership. Yet from the first day I came on board, it was all about management. I really don't know if they knew the difference or not . . . or cared!" (Rural school superintendent)

- "First time superintendents have no idea the frustration and challenge of the job. Unfortunately, I learned through experience. There should be an internship experience prior to accepting that first position." (Rural school superintendent)
- "There is a strong need for leadership but not sure I can provide what is necessary while faced with so many multi-tasking issues that must be addressed." (Small-city school superintendent)
- "I always felt more comfortable with the management part of the superintendency. Doing budgets, hiring staff, evaluating the principals, making sure the buses were on time, construction. I left the other stuff to both of the assistant superintendents." (Suburban school superintendent)
- "When it is all said and done, you better be good at both because if you aren't, someone will be out to get you—and eventually they will!" (Rural school superintendent)
- "I constantly find myself assessing my actions on serious matters. More reflective now than in the beginning." (Rural school superintendent)

REFLECTION

1. How do school leaders create meaningful understanding and appreciation for the problems associated with the dilemma of leadership versus management?
2. How can we know with certainty that we have adopted the most effective leadership/management approach?
3. In an educational system where accountability is important and is accompanied by many managerial tasks, what strategies can a school leader employ to ensure he or she finds time to be an effective leader?
4. What is the difference between leadership and management, and which is more effective for sustained success of a school organization?

SEVEN

Personal vs. Professional Life

Principle-centered people are not extremists—they do not make everything all or nothing. They do not divide everything into two parts, seeing everything as good or bad, as either/or. Their actions are proportionate to the situation—balanced, temperate, moderate, and wise.
—Stephen R. Covey

Part of my life is gone because I pursued the superintendency.
—Suburban school superintendent

In the classic 1946 movie *It's a Wonderful Life*, George Bailey is a man who has given up his hopes and dreams to save others, but has encountered some very difficult personal and professional issues. These issues drive George to the point of suicide on Christmas Eve, but he is saved by a "guardian angel," Clarence Odbody. Clarence shows George the impact he has had on his family and community, how he has touched the lives of so many, and how different life would be in the community if George had never been a part of it.

The responsibilities and problems inherent in the position of the superintendent of schools are wide in both scope and variety. Oftentimes, superintendents lead in a professional environment that is political, isolated, and demanding with little or no time for self-reflection. Unfortunately, there are few, if any, "guardian angels" to save school superintendents.

Because of the demands of the job, school superintendents do not take time, have the time, or even know how to reflect about the contributions that they have made both personally and professionally to education. And when the superintendent does have the time to reflect (usually late at night with no one around), there is a tendency to dwell on the negative not the positive. A number of superintendents suggested that "losing" was much harder to deal with and more personal than "winning." One superintendent stated:

> In one district, we were able to have bond issue pass that was not only the first one in several decades to pass, but had the potential to transform the district buildings and facilities. So we celebrated—for one night—and by the next morning, it was onto the next big issue. But, in another district, we tried to do a similar project and the voters soundly defeated it. And, not only did some of the board members constantly remind me of this "loss," but I did the same to myself. I constantly beat myself up, blamed myself, and became very hesitant to "stir the pot" anymore.

Studies have consistently shown that superintendents encounter considerable stress in their work that is directly related to their professional roles and personal responsibilities as the key leader of a school district. Glass and Franceschini (2007) reported that nearly 60 percent of superintendents across the country experienced levels of stress that were either considerable or very great. In addition, levels of stress for superintendents were, generally, greater those in other executive leadership positions.

In addition, Litchka, Fenzel, and Polka (2009) found that, overall, superintendents are quite vulnerable to the effects of stressors, most particularly role overload and role ambiguity. Furthermore, the study concluded that superintendents who indicated that they take steps to care for themselves (e.g., social activities, physical activities, spiritual activities, personal care) were better able to make decisions and solve problems. In addition, the impact that stress had on the superintendent when making decisions and solving problems appeared to have less impact on their personal life as well.

And so a dilemma exists in that superintendents may struggle with the balancing act between personal and professional life. With the kinds of decisions that a superintendent must make and problems that need to be solved, leaving decision-making and problem solving "at the office" does not often occur for many of these leaders. And on top of that, the impact of their actions would spill right into their personal lives.

Contemporary researchers such as Conger, Densten and Gray, and Rabey have concluded that because in-depth personal and professional reflection may challenge the favorable self-perceptions of many superintendents, a cycle develops whereby the superintendent runs the risk of making poor decisions and bad judgments similar to those of George Bailey in the *It's a Wonderful Life* story. In addition, Miller (2012) identified that self-reflection is most likely one of the superintendent's least favorite activities.

Others have stated that leaders avoid reflection because they are convinced by their past successes of their own invincibility, thus they fail to consider other perspectives regarding their professional and personal decisions and behaviors. Or that, to some, there is no time to do this. Just check this decision off and get onto the next one. This lack of reflection can have a negative impact on both their professional lives as well as their personal lives.

SUPERINTENDENT'S STORY:
ONE OR THE OTHER—BUT NOT BOTH

Jonathan Branson had lived the educator's dream life on the road to leadership. As a high school teacher, his energetic yet warm and caring style endeared him to the Burke High School students, peers, and the community. He coached sports. He sponsored clubs and activities. Within the first five years, he had become a department chair and then became the high school's assistant principal by the beginning of his seventh year at the school. It was during his fifth year of teaching that he began dating a fellow teacher, Sarah Dodd. They were married two years later, and within the next year, their first of three children, a son named Billy, was born.

Even after being appointed assistant principal, Jonathan's professional life continued to evolve and grow in stature. He firmly believed that he possessed acute knowledge about teaching and learning as well as unique interpersonal skills to make a difference in the way schools operated and how high school students were prepared for their future. Subsequently, he became immersed in curriculum development and instructional improvement processes and became a recognized advocate for student-centered changes at the high school level.

Jonathan's personal life was also starting to change in a significant way. Sarah gave birth to Billy and after that she took six months of maternity leave from her teaching. Jonathan was relieved that he had given up his high school coaching career so that he could spend more time at home with his wife and their new son. But soon he realized that the assistant principal position at the high school demanded that he spend additional time at school during the evenings and weekends supervising various student events. Although demanding of his time and energy, he still was convinced that educational administration provided him and his family with a pleasant life experience.

Sarah had resumed her teaching career when Billy was two years old but within another two years she had delivered another son, Freddie, and so again took a one-year leave of absence from teaching. Jonathan was able to continue to balance his expanded personal home life expectations with his role as assistant high school principal.

The school district administration, especially the assistant superintendent for curriculum and instruction continued to acknowledge and applaud Jonathan's accomplishments with various programs at the high school and as achievement test scores rose at Burke High School. The school district continued to use him as a consultant to the other schools in the district in terms of student-centered instruction and the use of technology to foster greater differentiation. He was well recognized in the school district as a trustworthy and respected curriculum-focused educational leader. And it became obvious to just about everyone in the school district that he was definitely in line for the next available secondary school principal position.

That career opportunity came to him as the newly constructed third high school of the district, Edgemont High School, was opened and he was appointed as its first high school principal in his eleventh year in education. Sarah had returned to teaching the year before as her two boys were both in elementary school at that time and she truly enjoyed resuming her career. However, within another year she was pregnant. As Jonathan finished his first year as principal he was now father of two boys and one girl. They agreed that Sarah would return to the classroom when their daughter, Amelia, was ready for daycare.

The central administration and school board members of the Woodshire Central School District were summarily impressed with Jonathan as a high school principal. He continued to find favor with his professional colleagues, faculty, and support staff because of his knowledge, skills, and dispositions related to school administration. The assistant superintendent encouraged Jonathan to pursue his doctorate at the university about fifty miles away from the school district. Jonathan was humbled but enthusiastic about this vote of confidence in his ability to continue to rise in his professional life.

He enrolled in the Ed.D. program and enjoyed getting involved with research projects related to school administration and the change process. At the university level Jonathan impressed his professors as well as his colleagues with his enthusiasm and motivation as well as his ability to get things done. He completed his Ed.D. in three years.

Sarah returned to teaching at the elementary school where she began over fifteen years previously. She had taken time off to raise her family and had only accumulated about six years into the district and state retirement system, whereas Jonathan had now accumulated over twenty years into the retirement system.

When Freddie was finishing middle school, Billy was in tenth grade, and Amelia was in third grade, another career opportunity presented itself to the Bransons. Jonathan was recommended for the position of assistant superintendent for curriculum and instruction at the Marshfield Central School District, a smaller suburban school district about twenty miles from the Branson's home in the Woodshire School District. After much debate between Jonathan and Sarah, it was decided that he would accept the position as it presented a wonderful professional opportunity for him but that they would keep their home in Woodshire so that their children could complete their education in that district where Sarah was now re-employed and where they had invested over two decades of their personal and professional lives.

Jonathan began his assistant superintendent for curriculum and instruction experience in this different district where he did not have a history or familiarity like he had in his previous school district. He was sometimes called "the outsider" by other "professionally jealous" administrators and faculty, but he reveled in the authority and the responsibilities that he had to impact curriculum and instruction.

His first couple of years went very well in terms of promoting curriculum and instructional changes pre-K through twelve but his strength was obviously at the secondary level where he was very much appreciated for his expertise. It took some time for him to gain the respect and acceptance at the elementary level but eventually the middle school teachers enjoyed his revitalization of the "middle school concept."

Jonathan found that the travel, or "windshield time" as he called it, to and from his home to his new school district was beginning to take a toll on him as he often was more fatigued than he had been in the past and because of his time commitments he was not able to spend as much time with his family as he previously did. The family joke in the Branson household was, "Is Dad coming home for dinner tonight?" with the answer being, "Yes, but he will be only about four hours late if tonight is an early night for him!" Sarah had a good blend of being a mom by being readily available to her own children as well as being in her own school setting and fulfilling much of her professional goals and ambitions. She was the mom in the stands at most of the children's school and sports events, whereas Jonathan tried his best to attend. It was not often possible due to work and traffic conditions.

Jonathan, however, felt that he was becoming more and more detached from his family as his work was consuming more of his time and energy. The relationship between Sarah and Jonathan entered an increasingly bumpy period. Jonathan and Sarah seemed to continue to drift apart in completely different professional and personal orbits. But fate dealt the Bransons another interesting professional and personal opportunity!

Martin Burns, the superintendent who hired Jonathan as a teacher and nurtured him as the high school principal at Woodshire Central School District, had budget and policy issues with the board of education and was abruptly dismissed at a regular board meeting in December. The board decided to post for a new superintendent of schools using a national consulting firm as a screening agency.

Sarah and Jonathan carefully debated whether or not he should apply for the position and return to his home school district. They agreed it would be fortuitous for them since now they would be able to resume a more normal family life and could truly enjoy being such an integral part of their school community again.

The only problematic issue that they could foresee was that Sarah would now be employed as a teacher in the same district that Jonathan would be the chief school officer and they could be subject to criticism because of the intertwining of their personal and professional lives. However, they agreed that the benefits outweighed the negatives and Jonathan applied for the superintendency.

He progressed through the process very well and the only concern expressed by the board was his spousal relationship. He was able to convince the board that he could separate the professional and personal aspects of his role as superintendent and if any situations arose where he thought there may be the slightest hint of favoritism he would recuse himself from the decision-making in that issue. He was selected by the board of education as the next superintendent of the Woodshire schools.

Once again, things ran somewhat smoothly for Jonathan for the first three years of his superintendency but a change in the board to a more fiscally conservative one as well as the election of some individuals who did not appreciate Jonathan's non-aggressive style of leadership in negotiations had an adverse impact on his relations with the board of education.

As the board was considering an extension on Jonathan's contract, it became obvious that some of the board members would just as soon not extend his contract, but since they were in the middle of protracted negotiations with the teachers' union, the board agreed that a limited extension was appropriate. The rift between various members of the board over Jonathan's continuation as superintendent was very frustrating for him as he felt that he had devoted several years of his remarkable professional career to this school district as a teacher, principal, and now superintendent of schools and he was being treated in this callous fashion.

It was hard for him to reconcile that even so many of his former colleagues, including teachers and administrators, were now viewing him as the "enemy" since he was the superintendent and could not assuage the board to reconsider its hard line approach to these contract negotiations that were impacting the climate and morale in the school district.

His acute professional knowledge, skills, and dispositions did not seem to have an impact on this board that seemed bent on "winning" the negotiations with the teachers first and then "going after" those high paid administrators next. Jonathan felt that his leadership was constantly being scrutinized from all stakeholders because of his wife's teaching position and the fact that two of his children still attended the schools of the district.

He felt the stress of trying to resolve the negotiations issues because he knew that this protracted conflict was not good for the district educationally nor was it good for his family personally. Both of his children would come home daily with stories about how their friends, whose parents were either teachers in the district or worked as educators at the university or in other contiguous districts, made negative comments about the state of the school district under the leadership of Dr. Branson.

Sarah had a difficult time at school as she tried to simply focus on teaching her second graders but her colleagues began to shun her because of her lack of support for their negotiations cause. She refused to participate in their union-directed demonstrations such as "working to rule"; "wearing black on Fridays"; "protesting at board meetings"; and "rallying at the town center."

The two years that this negotiations issue dragged on really took their toll on her as a professional as she tried not to let the union-organized efforts to assuage the board and her husband influence her demeanor and performance as a teacher, but it impacted her personally as she saw so many of her former friends and community associates drift away from her.

Jonathan's son Freddie and daughter Amelia had an even more difficult time adjusting to the ostracizing experiences they encountered from their friends and community groups because of this negotiations conflict. Both felt and openly expressed their disdain for the emotional heartaches that they believed they were forced to encounter because their father was the superintendent who could not resolve the conflict between the teachers and the board of education of the Woodshire School District.

Freddie was in his first years of high school, a very vulnerable and peer-oriented time period for him, and Amelia was in her final years of middle school, a time of intense physical and emotional changes anyway that were exacerbated by their real and/or perceived peer taunts and group pressures. It was a period of heightened anxiety for both of the Branson children who were still attending school in the district during this tumultuous time.

It has been said, "All good things must come to an end . . . and so too must all bad things" or as several sage members of the Woodshire School District astutely pontificated when this union versus school board acrimony began, "this too shall pass." And the negotiations did finally end.

The tipping point started to appear in earnest when the teachers issued a "work stoppage" or "strike" ultimatum to the board at the start of the new school year and scheduled it for the start of the fourth week of school that semester. Placards, posters, and radio and television "sound bites" articulated various components of the controversy in an aggressive political fashion to gain community support such as: the "Woodshire Teachers' Strike for Your Child's Education" or as the board pronounced, "There was simply no more money available to meet the union demands!"

Both sides seemed calcified in their positions while Superintendent Branson was caught in the middle trying to both manage the schools for academic achievement and manage the board for more rational decisions and behaviors relating to the negotiations.

His personal stress level was elevated to the extent that he needed to seek medical assistance for his elevated blood pressure because of the first hand experiences of these community-wide actions and behaviors upon his children. It was one thing to professionally deal with the negotiations but when he came home he got an earful from Sarah and his children, often lamenting that they would have all been better off had he stayed as assistant superintendent in the other school district and not brought this havoc to them.

The angst among the various stakeholders of Woodshire could be felt throughout the town as tensions between factions were at an all-time high. As the day of the "called strike" approached, tensions correspondingly increased to the "tipping point," and the board and the teachers' union held several long sessions to resolve their differences.

But as the strike was about to commence at Monday morning at 7:00 am, Jonathan was able to work a settlement at 6:30 am when he was able to assuage two of the board members to acquiesce to the teachers' perspective and resolve the negotiations by a vote of 4–3. But they were not happy with him for "prodding" them to do so, as they called it!

There was a sigh of relief throughout the community when the agreement was announced but the rift between the factions was solidified to the point that no one trusted anyone who was on the "wrong side" of this issue. The teachers' union was able to marshal community support for their negotiations in a very political fashion because they were activated to promulgate new candidates for election to the seven-member school board in order to change the "anti-teacher" attitude of the board and the community.

Time had again proved to be on the side of the teachers' union in this protracted controversy but time had engendered much stress on the part of key individuals on both sides of the negotiations table, especially on the superintendent of schools and two of his key supporters on the board of education who were subsequently defeated in their re-election bid. Two other board members who supported Jonathan's contract extension of the past also resigned prior to the election. They were disgusted with the situation and financially affected because their small businesses were adversely impacted by their political positions.

So as Jonathan personally reflected after the new board members were seated and the new teachers' contract was signed, "To me it appeared that there were more 'winners' than losers with this outcome but it doesn't bode well for me!"

However, Jonathan had two more years left on his contract and although he knew it would be a "rocky two years" he was willing to continue on the job and try to win favor with the new board of education and put into place some "healing" activities to also win back the support of the faculty, administration, and community.

His professional goal was to improve school district climate and employee morale in the post-acrimonious negotiations era but his personal goal was to survive in the superintendency as long as possible. But the professional stresses that he was continuing to experience on the job were only surpassed by the personal stresses that he was experiencing at home.

Sarah, Freddie, and Amelia were traumatized to various extents because of the role their father played in this controversy. It took Sarah some time to again feel that she "belonged" as a teacher in the district. There were overtures made to her by some faculty but she often felt that they were specious. She did continue to have a number of good relationships with some community members who she had known for decades but professionally she knew it would take time to overcome the enmity that this "almost strike" era had created for her.

Freddie was a high school junior who because of his participation in interscholastic and club athletic teams was able to redevelop trust and friendships with his peers, perhaps more because of his athletic prowess than anything else. But as he told his Dad, "I remember who really tried to 'bully me' during those negotiations days, and I 'see' them in the opposition every time I am called upon in an athletic contest!" He had turned this situation into a positive motivator for himself and it worked as he became well renowned in the region as a scholar-athlete.

Amelia, now a freshman at high school, was having the most difficult time resuming her social and emotional stability in the post-negotiations era as she had a more limited social group of friends and as her father identified, "They were not the most inspiring group of high school students—some of them having been introduced to him as superintendent in the past for disciplinary reasons."

Jonathan was truly concerned for her and carefully watched for signs of substance abuse; unfortunately, his assumptions based on his experiences were correct as she needed additional emotional and psychological support to overcome some substance-related problems. She always seemed to have more "guy friends" than "girl friends" around her and she enjoyed their attention and was attracted to their rebellious orientation. But Jonathan was able to arrange for excellent counseling for her and she seemed to be re-adjusting to life as a high school teenager, albeit one whose father is the superintendent of schools.

Jonathan had been pondering a possible career move to another part of the state to relieve his family of some of this personal stress but he met stern resistance from each of them as he announced his intention to consider another superintendency. Sarah was immutable in her opposition to any move at this time. He was taken aback by her rebuke to his suggestion:

> I have given up much of my teaching career so that we could have a family and live in this community where I have had family roots for generations. I want to work until I am vested for retirement purposes and I want to teach in Woodshire because it's where I know and I live. I believe that my teaching excellence will eventually eliminate any vestiges of that negotiation fiasco among my colleagues. And, I think it's best for our children to finish their schooling here! If you want to move — go ahead and move but we won't go with you!

Freddie was a little more cavalier but practical in his response to his father's proposal, "Dad, do what you think is best for you — but, I need to stay in Woodshire to graduate. I can't go with you for the next two years and then I'll be away at college like Billy and away from it ALL!"

Amelia, after some loud emotional outbursts and hysteria, finally stated that she was planning on staying in Woodshire no matter what. "And, if this family leaves I may just 'drop out of school,' like I was thinking about anyway, and move in with one of my boy friends."

Jonathan was shocked that after all his family had been through in this community they didn't want to leave it. They felt that their roots were firmly planted in Woodshire and they wanted to stay put. But as this superintendent career experience was evolving he also was becoming much more reflective about his professional educational successes and the choices and subsequent personal sacrifices he made to help others succeed, especially students and teachers.

As he reflected, he identified that perhaps the greatest professional excitements for him occurred when he could resolve issues by working collaboratively with others. His view was that without him that strike might have occurred and the community would be even more divided than it is today. He ruminated that now he was experiencing a different kind of "high-touch" emotional rollercoaster with and against some of his board members and the focus was not on him leading, teaching, and learning but more on personal grudges and for his professional survival.

There was a time that, like George Bailey in *It's a Wonderful Life*, he felt that it may have been better if he had never become a superintendent or perhaps had simply stayed as the successful high school principal at Burke High School. He did not have a guardian angel like Clarence to "talk some reflective sense to him" but he did have two good mentors who helped him navigate through this complex personal and professional crisis by reviewing the impact that he has had on various people, things, and ideas of education in this region. They used a summary evaluation process similar to that exemplified best in the movie *Mr. Holland's Opus*, where at the twilight of his career it became obvious that he had, indeed, made a big difference in the lives of several people.

Jonathan was gratified with the imagery employed by his mentor, former superintendent Harris, who even re-watched the movie with him over a couple of beers to promote this deep reflection. He said that a mentor had done the same to him several years before and it helped him through one of his personal and professional crises. This directed reflection definitely helped Jonathan as he thought he heard bells ringing that night. He began to think of his next professional moves but well within the context of his personal life!

Jonathan Branson's story is not unique to superintendents. These educational leaders often find themselves "on the horns" of personal and professional dilemmas in which making decisions can have profound consequences for them. Superintendents need to be aware of such real "lived experiences" so that they may better prepare themselves and others for the personal and professional costs of being an educational leader in contemporary America. One superintendent noted:

> This personal versus professional life is the only area where I treated myself differently from my co-workers and subordinates. I ask all of my employees to "put family first," because if they come to work worrying about a loved one at home, their head won't be in the right place on the job. When it came to me, however, work always came first. I missed every major event in my own children's lives. I tell all my administrators to use Stephen Covey's concept of "sharpening the saw" (1989). Spend time with family. Take time to exercise and relax. But, looking back, I was not a good model for this advice.

Surviving the personal versus professional dilemma can be a daunting task for a superintendent. While many of these leaders have learned to think, act, and behave in a linear, rational, and logical manner, often it is very difficult for them to be able to deal with either the personal or professional impact their decision-making can have. Worse yet, it can be much more difficult—or impossible—for these leaders when *both* their personal and professional lives are affected in such a manner.

A number of superintendents, when faced with the personal versus professional dilemma, stated that they would rather "go it alone" than create alliances. Some said that they were afraid to collaborate with others since the partner may have their own ideas that may be in conflict with yours, resulting in a needless waste of time in which the process slows down. And so they did everything possible by themselves, even if it meant longer days (and nights).

Ironically, a number of superintendents were reluctant to share power with others for fear it would take away from the perception that "I am in charge . . . I am responsible." Going in a more collaborative direction could send a message to the board that perhaps the superintendent was not as competent as they thought or expected.

The qualitative interviews associated with this research study also reconfirmed the key issues related to making decisions and solving problems while "living on the horns of dilemmas." Therefore, it is imperative that superintendents of schools spend time reflecting on their leadership decisions and their contributions to the profession and their respective communities especially in light of the personal impact of time and stress that this professional leadership position involves.

Most times, superintendents are not as fortunate as George Bailey to have a guardian angel to provide a safety net for them. And some superintendents have become "lost" in their personal and professional lives, due to the stressors associated with their leadership and decision-making roles. However, one could start by following the advice of Stephen Covey, who suggested that "sharpening the saw" in the personal and professional areas of physical, emotional, spiritual, and social well-being is an excellent place to start. This could be, in fact, the guardian angel that many have been looking for as they deal with the dilemmas of decision-making.

Therefore, this sample's participants identified that the superintendency is challenging, time consuming, and stressful to one's physical and emotional health as well as family relationships as reflected in the above story of Jonathan Branson. But we all need to keep in mind that it truly is "A wonderful life. . . . Isn't it?" As one long-time superintendent reiterated, "You're damn right it is!"

VOICES FROM THE ARENA

Scholars

- "What lies behind us and what lies before us are tiny matters compared to what lies within us." (Oliver Wendell Holmes)
- "The personal power that comes from principle-centered living is the power of a self-aware, knowledgeable, proactive individual, unrestricted by attitudes, behaviors, and actions of others or by many of the circumstances and environmental influences that limit other people." (Stephen Covey)
- "There is no real excellence in all this world which can be separated from right living." (David Starr Jordan)
- "One of the most important ways to manifest integrity is to be loyal to those who are not present." (Stephen Covey)
- "Service is the rent we pay for the privilege of living on this earth." (N. Eldon Tanner)
- "In an effort to reach the heart of others, one must speak from the heart." (Doris Kearns-Goodwin)

- "With public sentiment, nothing can fail, without it nothing can succeed." (Abraham Lincoln)
- "To be what we are, and to become what we are capable of becoming is the only end in life." (Robert Louis Stevenson)
- "Power tends to corrupt; absolute power corrupts absolutely." (Lord Acton)
- "So much to do, so little done." (Cecil Rhodes)
- "Well done is always more important than well said." (Benjamin Franklin)
- "Is it better to be feared than loved?" (Niccolò Machiavelli)
- "I learned not from those who taught me, but those who talked with me." (St. Augustine)
- "In general, the more emotionally demanding the work, the more empathic and supportive the leader needs to be." (Daniel Goleman)
- "Transformational change starts first in our minds . . . because the way we think determines how we feel, the way we feel determines how we act significantly determines whether or not transformation is achieved." (Francis Duffy)

Practicing Superintendents

- "First time superintendents have no idea the frustration and challenge of the job. Unfortunately, I learned through experience." (Rural school superintendent)
- "The job is stressful. Overload of work resulting in fatigue, loss of sleep. A lot of sleepless nights." (Small-city school superintendent)
- "People going into the position must understand the demands. It is literally 24/7." (Suburban school superintendent)
- "Some boards treat you like the hired hand and expect you to be on the job all day, every day." (Rural school superintendent)
- "I try not to take the job home, but eventually while at home I begin to think about it." (Suburban school superintendent)
- "I got calls from the board president on Sunday mornings asking me what I was going to do about this or that . . . or did I read about so-and-so in the paper . . . and what was I going to do about it!" (Small-city school superintendent)
- "I literally and figuratively became a 'BEAR' to live with. I could not walk away from the demands of the superintendency; it was constantly on my mind like a first love but without mutual personal gratification!" (Rural school superintendent)

REFLECTION

1. How far are we—as superintendents—able to act as free agents in pursuing opportunity and happiness not only for ourselves but for our family as well, while serving in a leadership capacity as superintendent of schools?
2. Lincoln was advised that upon his inauguration as president that he was "now public property and ought to be where he can be reached by the people." Does this statement apply to the school superintendency as well? If so, under what conditions?
3. Life as a school superintendent can be pretty hectic at times, so much so that you fail to find time for yourself or your family. How might you strike a balance in your personal life and your professional life?
4. To maintain the work/life balance as a school leader, what fundamental questions do you need to ask yourself? For example: Why did you choose to become a superintendent of schools? What areas of your personal/professional role are irreplaceable? What would you like your life to be like in ten years?

EIGHT
Matador de Toros!

Of course there is no formula for success, except perhaps an uncondi-
tional acceptance of life, and what it brings.
—Arthur Rubinstein

Perhaps no writer has brought more attention to bullfighting than Ernest
Hemingway. Following the publication of two of his most famous works,
The Sun Also Rises (1926) and *A Farewell to Arms* (1929), Hemingway
would spend the summer of 1929 researching and writing a discourse on
bullfighting. *Death in the Afternoon* (1932) provides an acute account of the
pageantry, magnificence, and intensity of the "sport" of bullfighting.
Consider Hemingway's astute observation about bullfighting from *Death
in the Afternoon*:

> It is one hundred to one against the matador de toros being killed
> unless he is inexperienced, ignorant, out of training or too old and
> heavy on his feet. But the matador, if he knows his profession, can
> increase the amount of the danger of death that he runs exactly as
> much as he wishes. It is to his discredit if he runs danger through
> ignorance, through disregard of the fundamental rules, through physi-
> cal or mental slowness, or through blind folly.

We present the metaphor of bullfighting for several reasons. We contend that being a superintendent of schools—particularly during the past
several decades—can be like the matador facing the bull in the arena,
particularly when making decisions of significance and urgency. The bull
has two horns, is much heavier and stronger than the matador, and the
matador, to be successful, must make great use of knowledge, science,
and absolute bravery in order to put on a public performance and win the
battle and not be either killed or disgraced (Hemingway would argue
that the former is better for the matador than the latter!).

93

While we do not suggest that the superintendent faces physical death while making such decisions, several superintendents shared that the professional "death" of their respective tenure at a district or the potential imminent end of a well-established career was attributable to the decision-making approaches they employed to resolve key school district dilemmas. The metaphor of the matador could be viewed from the following perspective:

- The bull (board of education) is much stronger than the matador (superintendent), who is often left in the middle of the ring (public arena) with little more than a sword (leadership knowledge and skills) and a cape (personal dispositions) to advocate his decisions, protect his professional integrity, and deflect negative attention.
- More than one bull (board of education, community, teachers' union, parents) may be charging at the matador (superintendent) at the same time. There are so many decision-making dilemmas that educational leaders face on a regular basis that superintendents must possess a ubiquitous alertness to see where in the arena the current horns are located and from whence future horns may emerge.
- In order to be successful, the matador (superintendent) must be at his best—physically, emotionally, and intellectually—to artfully and skillfully confront the "horns of the bulls" so that the outcome is favorable to the leader and meets the approval of those watching in the arena (school board members, administrators, faculty, students, parents, and community members).
- The bull(s) may never have been in the ring before, and as a result, the matador (superintendent) may be facing an unpredictable, angry, and out-of-control opponent who would like nothing more than to reverse the superintendent's decision, take away his authority (sword) and professional integrity (cape), and force him to succumb to pressure from the crowd in the arena.

And so while some may submit that this may be a bit of a stretch, we listened to many superintendents who were put "in the ring" by themselves—to defend their position and not lose the battle but also to keep their honor! And so we offer the following acronym—M.A.T.A.D.O.R.— as a guide for superintendents as they venture into the dangerous arena of decision-making, using words of advice from the leadership literature and research including from the many superintendents that we interviewed and observed during our careers.

MISSION—FOCUS ON POSSIBLE AND PREFERABLE OUTCOMES

Successful leaders focus their personal and professional time, energy, and resources on accomplishing the long-term goals and short-term objectives of their respective organizations. They continuously reflect about their various daily actions and key decisions as relates to moving the various elements of the organization toward successfully completing the various tasks and projects associated with those identified goals and objectives.

Successful leaders are knowledgeable about the current status of their organization; they know the "brutal realities" as Collins suggests in *Good to Great*, but they have a vision and a sense of mission of how to improve their organization by their development in their subordinates, employees, and clients of an acute sense of "commitment" to do better in their various benchmarks on the road to accomplishing their mission and vision.

Brown and Moffett (1992) contend that sharing the mission and gaining support throughout the organization is the key to educational leadership success when they offer, "Through a shared mission, we can work together to find viable answers to the riddles of chaos and complexity troubling educators, students, parents, and community members." They apply organizational resources and human capital energy to "keep marching towards accomplishing the vision," as Robert Kennedy offered with the famous statement from George Bernard Shaw, "Some people see things as they are and say: why? I dream things that never were and say: why not?"

However, successful leaders are also realists who not only know the brutal realities of their current situation, but also know that "an organization's collective grasps should always exceed its reach" and that although the vision is the ideal, to accomplish various aspects of it along the way and celebrate those successes are important for the morale and support of the followers. Consequently, successful leaders, like very good bull fighters, know that the preferable outcome may not be obtained (don't kill all the bulls) but there are possible and probable mission outcomes that continue the progression to the intended vision but are not so final (the bull is succumbed but not eliminated).

The artful superintendent constantly articulates the vision to all stakeholders and applauds and/or encourages those in the arena to applaud key benchmark successes and those who contributed to them along the mission journey.

Several contemporary leadership authors accentuate the value of mission-driven leadership in all kinds of organizations including schools. Wes Roberts, author of *Leadership Secrets of Attila the Hun* (1985) and *Make It So: Leadership Secrets from Star Trek: The Next Generation* (1995), contends that having the sense of mission is the most important leadership characteristic. He references examples of individuals who had an incredible sense of mission and when given specific tasks related to the mission were anxious and able to "just do it" so that they could move their respective organization component along on its path to the preferable vision.

As a matter of fact, as school district leaders are well aware, ELCC (2008) Standard #1 that forms the basis for most educational leadership programs in the United States is: "Facilitating the development, articulation, implementation and stewardship of a district vision of learning that is shared and supported by the school community."

Therefore, mission and vision are considered the most important elements for a successful school district leader from a theoretical formative perspective. This leadership focus resonates with what Kouzes and Posner (2007) offer: "No matter what it is called . . . personal agenda, legacy, dream, goal, or vision . . . the intent is the same. Leaders must be forward looking and have a clear sense of direction that they want to take the organization." They must exude a confidence about their belief and commitment to the mission and the future of their organization.

Fullan (2006) reiterates this confidence in the mission and vision: "Leaders need to convey confidence about the future even though they are not (should not be) fully certain." Accordingly, Daniel Goleman (2002) advocates a specific practice to do such: "Begin each small-group meeting with a reminder of why they were in business . . . their vision, values, and mission."

Additionally, several leadership gurus have comprehensively explored the significance of having a sense of mission and the problems that beset the organization if the leader does not possess the sense of mission that is congruent with followers. Covey (1989) advocated that, "your mission statement becomes your constitution, the solid expression of your vision and values. It becomes the criterion by which you measure everything else in life."

On the other hand, Bennis and Nanus (1985) argued that vision is important but it needs to be virtuous as well, stating, "Competence, or knowledge, without vision and virtue, breeds technocrats. Virtue, without vision and knowledge, breeds ideologues. Vision without virtue and knowledge breeds demagogues." And Max DePree (1989) submits

> Closely related to this are the problems that surface when we lose sight of who we are and why we are here. Leaders cannot afford to lose track of the present. I often think of the apostolic zeal of leaders like Mohandas Gandhi and Albert Schweitzer. They knew where they stood and where they wanted to go and, especially, who they needed to be.

Contemporary school superintendents, like bullfighters, need to know where they personally and professionally stand, where their vision and mission will lead them, and how they need to perform while in the arena so the crowds cheer and return to applaud their successes again! Practicing superintendents echo the significance of having a mission and a vision to succeed in the school leadership arena:

- "My job [as superintendent] is to set the tone . . . what is expected . . . how we meet the vision and mission of the school district." (Rural school superintendent)
- "There was a philosophical disconnect. 'Good is good enough' by the board president. There was a need to challenge the board on 'Good is good enough.'" (Suburban school superintendent)
- "People are angry. People need to learn to work together or we will not survive." (Rural school superintendent)
- "It took two years to develop a mission and vision statements. And from these we got a commitment and programs that reflected these statements. Yet this took a couple of years as well." (Rural school superintendent)

AWARENESS—VIGILANT ABOUT MICRO AND MACRO CONTEXTS

The school superintendent is the leadership individual of the school district charged with the responsibility for the effective and efficient education of all of the children within the community. The school superintendent is in the community "gold fish bowl" 24/7 and is as Abraham Lincoln posited, "public property." The personal and professional actions, reactions, decisions, and outcomes associated with the district are a reflection of the superintendent in the eyes of the public.

The matador is symbolic of the bullfight in the arena and just the thought of him conjures up thoughts of the pageantry, elegance, artfulness, and the emotional rollercoaster associated with the event. Like the bullfighter, superintendents wear their performances on their respective sleeves throughout their tenure in the district. They become known for their dress, their interactive style, their idiosyncratic behaviors, their relationships, and their impacts on the onlookers.

The successful superintendents whom we have known and with whom we have discussed leadership issues have specifically identified the importance of being aware of the who, what, when, where, why, and how impact the various people, things, and ideas in the context of the school and, also, the relationships of those in the school district context. Several superintendents related that perhaps the most important of the national standards for educational leaders might be the one standard that is least understood, Standard #6: "Understanding, responding to, and influencing the larger political, social, economic, legal, and cultural context" (2008).

Superintendents, like bullfighters, need to be aware of where the "bulls with their sharp horns" are located, what movements or actions will get them riled, which ones will wear them out, and, of course, what pleases the crowds in the arena the most and what causes them to be indifferent and unsupportive.

Context matters, as do personal and professional relationships in terms of being a successful leader in contemporary school systems. Goleman (2002) emphasizes the importance of contextual awareness when he offers,

> A leader with a keen social awareness sense can be politically astute, able to detect crucial social networks and read key power relationships. Such leaders can understand the political/social forces at work as well as guiding values and unspoken rules that operate among people.

Superintendents who are astutely aware as leaders have developed a "sixth sense" similar to the classroom teacher who seems to have "eyes in back of her head" and knows what it is happening in the context at all times. Psychologist Robert Slavin (1998) refers to this as "teacher with-it-ness."

We contend that successful district-wide leaders also possess a "leadership with-it-ness" similar to that "with-it-ness" of the effective teacher that enables them to ferret out the various factors that may be hazardous to their superintendency. Such superintendents possess the same attribute that the astute bullfighters possess in knowing when and where to attack which bulls and when not to do so, while also maintaining their arena-wide perspective on the reactions of the onlookers and other potential charging bulls.

However, it needs to be emphasized that the contexts in which superintendents work reflect a constantly changing environment that is continually impacted from external macro-level demands and expectations such as federal and state education policies and accountability approaches. Successful superintendents also develop an acute awareness of the delicate balance between people, things, and ideas that contribute to organizational satisfaction and productivity (Polka et al., 2013).

Like bullfighters who recognize that every bull and every fight is a different experience, wise superintendents recognize that every board of education meeting, election, budget referendum, contract negotiation, and policy decision is a unique experience. Accordingly, successful school leaders are "keenly aware of the continual dance they are in with their present capacity, the emerging conditions that surround them, and the future that lies before them" (Klimek et al., 2008).

Consequently, the superintendent is a voracious learner who is well versed in the people, things, and ideas of the ever-evolving context and is a perpetual teacher who articulates the district policies and procedures with a focus on mission and vision. Such a superintendent is akin to the Mark Twain (1886) perspective of the Mississippi River boat pilot:

Two things seemed pretty apparent to me. One was that in order to be a Mississippi River pilot, a man had got to learn more than any one man ought to be allowed to know; and the other was that he must learn it all over again in a different way every 24 hours.

Indeed, a contemporary superintendent should know more about the school district than any one person ought to know and he or she must learn it all over again every day! Awareness is definitely a critical component of school leadership success.

Superintendents from our experiences have suggested the following about possessing acute awareness:

- "Always ASK yourself if the proposed change is good for children, and if you can defend it in a public forum. Both answers need to be . . . YES." (Suburban school superintendent)
- "You are the BIG FISH in the district goldfish bowl—and people are always watching when and how you swim and with whom you are swimming—be sure that you are always aware of where you are and with whom you are swimming!" (Suburban school superintendent)
- "We need to be honest with respect to our performance and the performance of others on staff." (Rural school superintendent)
- "At times you may promote conflict, not deep anxiety conflict, but just enough to get everyone's attention." (Small-city school superintendent)
- "District was in turmoil. Complete disconnect with the community. Several key administrators left the district. There was a need to provide authoritarian leadership to keep the board from micromanaging." (Suburban school superintendent)
- "I have moved toward alignment in regards to district projects. More structure. Less creativity. Test results are the bottom line." (Small-city school superintendent)
- "Building consensus is stressful." (Small-city school superintendent)
- "There is a strong need for leadership . . . not power trips. Having a respectful relationship with others is critical." (Rural school superintendent)
- "You will always be in trouble when you try to make significant change." (Suburban school superintendent)

TENACITY—PERSISTENCE TO COMPLETE TASKS WITH ETHICAL COHESIVENESS

Superintendents who confided in us about their trials, tribulations, and thrills of leading school districts also expressed an immutable belief in their personal and professional values and ethical approaches to decision-making and problem solving. Superintendents we interviewed strongly felt that ELCC Standard #5, "Acting with integrity, fairness, and in an ethical manner," was a key factor for surviving and thriving in the position. They steadfastly maintained their ethical principles and, in the face of adversity, refused to be compromised or make deals to survive crises.

Superintendents maintained an idealized influence upon others because of their ethical orientation as advocated by Marzano, Waters, and McNulty (2005): "Idealized influence is characterized by modeling behavior through exemplary personal achievements, character, and behavior." They continued to "do what is right" for the good of the organization even though they may have been jeopardizing their own career.

These leaders possess a cohesive connection between their core values and their leadership souls that Bolman and Deal (1991) would support. This disposition is frequently reflected in their decision-making approaches no matter the dilemma they are facing. Such superintendents are the role models that Hall and Hord (2006) advocate: "The superintendent should understand and model appropriate value systems, ethics, and moral leadership." Just like the bullfighter who does not waver when facing the bull but considers all of his options, the superintendents expressed their commitment to integrity, fairness, and acting in an ethical manner.

Several of the superintendents we interviewed expressed much dismay at a few of their colleagues who succumbed to unethical practices and/or made proverbial "deals with the devils" so they could continue in their leadership positions. They felt that those individuals were often spotlighted by the ever-present media and caused inordinate damage to the office of the school superintendent. They became the well-known examples of leaders who committed major leadership faux pas that resulted in a public distrust and even abhorrence of the chief school officer position.

Such "fallen leaders" experienced a significant loss of the cohesion between their mind, heart, and soul as appropriately expressed by Bolman and Deal (1995): "Leaders who have lost touch with their own soul, who are confused and uncertain about their core values and beliefs inevitably lose their way."

Superintendents reiterated that all those currently in the position as well as those aspiring to the position need to possess an enthusiastic appreciation for the "office of the superintendent" and its quintessential role as the champion of education for all. They felt that school district leaders "need to be the kind of change they want to see in the world" à la Gandhi and that they need to remain ever-faithful to the key ethical principles and human values that have been the foundation of the position since the first superintendent became the educational leader in Buffalo, New York in 1837.

Also, district leaders have the responsibility to embed this ethical orientation into all levels of their organization so that the sense of moral purpose does not only reside in the superintendent's office: "Not only must moral purpose guide and drive our efforts, but moral purpose must also go beyond individual heroism to the level of a system quality" (Fullan, 2003).

Covey reinforces the inherent value during decision-making to keep a focus on key principles and maintain an exuberant tenacity to be ethical when he stated, "Our behavior is a function of our decisions, not our conditions. We can subordinate feelings to values. We have the initiative and responsibility to make things happen." Bolman and Deal (2005) concur about the need for superintendents to be tenacious in their leadership in contemporary schools:

> We need leaders and managers who appreciate that management is a deeply moral and ethical undertaking. We need leaders who combine hardheaded realism with a deep commitment to values and purpose larger than themselves.

Possessing tenacity was often referred to by superintendents:

- "It took four years before things started to come together." (Suburban school superintendent)
- "Keep in mind what is really important, make decisions that support your moral compass." (Rural school superintendent)
- "The superintendent's chair has a high moral ground . . . never give it up because of dishonest behavior. Do the right thing." (Suburban school superintendent)
- "We are at a crossroads in education. People just do not get it. We need to continue to address the issues." (Small-city school superintendent)
- "I was the last person standing." (Suburban school superintendent)
- "The position of superintendent today is a volatile position . . . will you be able to meet the challenges for a long period of time? The job will take a personal toll on you and your family." (Small-city school superintendent)
- "The buck stops with the superintendent. You need to realize that you are the last word when necessary." (Suburban school superintendent)
- "Stand for what is important." (Suburban school superintendent)
- "It takes time to build trust, critical for change to happen." (Rural school superintendent)

- "It is so hard to keep balance to encourage creativity and collaboration and still meet agreed upon goals." (Rural school superintendent)

ASTUTE—BEING DISCERNING AND WISE IN DECISION-MAKING

According to ELCC (2008) Standard #3, educational leaders have the professional responsibility of "ensuring management of the organization, operations, and resources for a safe, efficient, and effective learning environment." In discussing this role responsibility with superintendents, we found that they are focused on providing the most effective learning environment for the students of their school districts.

Superintendents recognize that there are several intervening variables that impact the deployment of the resources of their respective school districts to do so. There never seems to be enough people, money, or time to provide for the learning needs and interests of all students within the expectations of the faculty, administration, parents, and community.

Superintendents expressed to us that they are constantly trying to find the appropriate balance between the program needs of all learners and the fiscal expectations of the community. The search for that delicate balance is a never-ending quest of school superintendents as those program needs and community expectations change on an irregular basis.

It takes a very discriminating leadership disposition and a wise approach to decision-making on the part of the school district leader to find that appropriate balance on a regular basis and prominently communicate to the various school district stakeholders. Again the superintendent, as the educational leader of the school district, like the matador in the arena, performs the roles expected within a continually changing paradigm based on various factors over which he or she has little or no control, like the aggressiveness of the bulls on a particular day.

Superintendents related to us that they rely on their professional reflections based on their previous experiences within their leadership contexts and make decisions after careful analysis of all the extenuating circumstances that impact their current reality. Like matadors, superintendents are very astute in their decision-making and use a variety of problem-solving approaches to appropriately find that "delicate balance" for their school districts at the specific time.

The decision-making approaches may vary but our research has concluded that superintendents use the decision-making process that they believe is most appropriate to solve the particular issue, including such decision-making models as: 1) Classical, 2) Incremental, 3) Garbage Can, 4) Shared Decision-Making, 5) Satisficing, 6) Mixed Scanning, and 7) Political (Polka et al., 2013).

However, whichever approach is selected to solve the ever-present dilemmas associated with contemporary school district leadership, the superintendent needs to astutely determine which process and outcome are most appropriate at the time to effectively and efficiently resolve the issue. The superintendents perform these decisions based on their reflections of past similar situations and their assessment of the current context and the future outcomes, just as bullfighters do in their arenas.

And the onlookers are ubiquitous, watching every move with anxious anticipation and personal expectations that the outcomes will be favorable to them because, after all, they do pay for the performance! Wise superintendents recognize this aspect of their public leadership position and perform accordingly and astutely in the execution of their decision-making duties.

But this discernment disposition within a public arena is not often formally taught to aspiring superintendents. Most identified that they learned this disposition over time in the position and with the help of key mentors who provided them with sage advice as various decision-making issues arose in their school districts. Our advice to aspiring superintendents is to find a wise mentor or two and reflect upon their advice during the early years of your superintendency so that you make wise decisions, especially related to finding that ever-elusive balance between program needs and community expectations in this age of heightened accountability.

Still leadership astuteness can be learned, as several contemporary leadership researchers have illustrated in their reviews of various key components of this disposition. Michael Fullan (2001) relates that the mindset of the leader has much to do with the development of this disposition when he writes, "Understanding the change process is less about innovation and more about innovativeness. It is less about strategy and more about strategizing." And Robert Greene (1998) agrees that leaders need to be astute in their approach to change in schools when he advises, "Preach the need for change, but never reform too much at once."

Superintendents shared the following regarding the ability to be discerning:

- "Net-working with staff is important. Must build strong creditable, respectful relations." (Small-city school superintendent)
- "It helps to develop an entry plan. The entry plan provides you with an opportunity to hit the ground running. It helps to better understand the culture as well as determine where the problems exist." (Suburban school superintendent)
- "You must be able to sort out the implications of a decision." (Suburban school superintendent)
- "Listen! Listen! Listen! It is 50% of the communication process." (Suburban school superintendent)

- "Find out sooner rather than later what the non-negotiable items are." (Suburban school superintendent)
- "You must be able to recognize self-serving issues . . . yours as well as others." (Rural school superintendent)
- "The rules are clear in public education." (Suburban school superintendent)
- "To create dynamic tension is the ultimate balancing act." (Small-city school superintendent)
- "The job is not about having the right answers all the time, but asking the right questions." (Rural school superintendent)
- "Ask—don't answer." (Suburban school superintendent)

DETERMINATION—RESOLUTENESS IN DECISION-MAKING AND PROBLEM SOLVING

Superintendents like bullfighters need to possess a controlled yet indomitable belief in the correctness of their decisions while they are performing in the arena. Superintendents expressed to us that it is extremely essential for success in the position to focus on ELCC Standard #2, "Advocating, nurturing, and sustaining a school culture and instructional program conducive to student learning and staff professional growth." As the chief school officer of the school district, the superintendent is expected to be the educational leader of the community and make decisions that promote the development of the curriculum and the improvement of the instruction.

Superintendents use data to drive their decisions related to educational achievement decisions in their school districts. They follow the advice of Collins and Hansen (2011), who emphasize that effective leaders, "do not look to conventional wisdom to set their course, nor do they primarily look to what other people do, or what the pundits or experts say what they should do. They look at empirical evidence."

However, superintendents also cautioned that making decisions that effectuate program changes in contemporary schools engenders resistance from various stakeholders who are comfortable with "the way that things have always been done around here." Superintendents also responded that in promulgating major educational changes they often felt like they were living the Myth of Sisyphus as recorded by Albert Camus (1942) wherein, "The gods condemned Sisyphus to ceaselessly rolling a rock to the top of a mountain, whence the stone would fall back of its own weight, subsequently resulting in futile and hopeless labor."

In addition, the superintendents expressed the leadership concerns of Peter Senge (1990) when he wrote, "We all know what it feels like to be facing compensating feedback, the harder you push, the harder the system pushes back; the more effort you expend trying to improve matters, the more effort seems to be required." But successful superintendents never give up their quest to improve the educational program of their system and eventually their determined efforts for educational improvements are sustained.

Collins and Hansen (2011) agree that being resolute in decision-making and problem solving are requisites of leaders whose organizations are exemplary. They advise leaders to behave as effective bullfighters and develop the will power to reject pressures to conform in ways incompatible with their values, performance standards, and long-standing aspirations. They contend that successful leaders must possess a determined disposition like, "having the inner will to do whatever it takes to create a great outcome, no matter how difficult." This advice is congruent with that offered by the English philosopher John Ruskin (2012), who proclaimed, "Quality is never an accident . . . it is always the result of intelligent effort, but, there must be the will to produce a superior product."

Superintendents who participated in our research studies have consistently agreed that to be effective in advocating, nurturing, and sustaining a school culture and instructional program conducive to student learning and staff professional growth, the onus is on the leader to be resolute in decision-making related to making changes and possess a determined will to make improved quality happen.

Being resolute in decision-making and problem solving was suggested numerous times by superintendents:

- "Stand for what is important. Address the issues. It is your responsibility to do so. If unable, perhaps it is time to get out of the kitchen." (Small-city school superintendent)
- "I have a strong belief in educating kids . . . anything that deters or undermines the process . . . I will take a stand . . . it is that simple." (Rural school superintendent)
- "Must stay focused on what we are doing to continue to improve quality education for all . . . not on the personal issues of difficult board members." (Small-city school superintendent)
- "We need to get away from relying on demographics and do the job. Too often demographics are used as an excuse for poor student achievement." (Small-city school superintendent)
- "There is a need to know what your core values are." (Suburban school superintendent)
- "Patience, watch, listen, and learn. Find something to celebrate." (Rural school superintendent)
- "Such a disconnect . . . social agency vs. an educational agency. The board preferred the former." (Suburban school superintendent)

OPTIMISM—ENTHUSIASTIC PERSPECTIVE
OF POSITIVE OUTCOMES

Bullfighters do not enter into the arena with a negative attitude regarding the outcome of their performance and neither do school superintendents. A number of superintendents have emphatically expressed to us the significance of leaders having enthusiastic positive perspectives about the outcomes of their various decisions. Accordingly, they advocate that effective leaders exude a confident attitude about the results of projects, strategies, and activities that they endorse. They follow the leadership admonishment of leadership guru Robert Greenleaf (1997) who stated, "One can make too optimistic assumptions and suffer endless frustration or too pessimistic ones and curb one's operations."

Yet one must err on the side of optimism and accept the frustration. Collins (2011) concurs with this positive orientation as his researcher team identified the significance of the Stockdale Paradox, which posits that leaders retain absolute faith that they can and will prevail in the end, regardless of the difficulties, and at the same time, they must confront the most brutal facts of their current reality, whatever they might be.

Superintendents identified that this prevailing positive attitude with honest recognition of potential negative factors is very important when school leaders employ the concepts associated with ELCC Standard #4: "Collaborating with families and community members, responding to diverse community interests and needs, and mobilizing community resources." Superintendents contend that parents and community must perceive that the leader believes that proposed education program changes will result in positive outcomes for the school district. It has been articulated that an optimistic attitude becomes infectious and can definitely contribute to leadership success of superintendents as they motivate others to overcome obstacles to change.

School district leaders need to be zealous in their optimism when collaborating with various stakeholders. All subordinates look to the leader for clues as to the potential success of various planned actions and decisions. The superintendent must be the pinnacle of optimism for board of education members, other district and building administrators, faculty, parents, students, and community members no matter the issue or the specific interest bias of the group vis-à-vis the planned change.

While not easy, effective superintendents customize their presentations, interactions, and communications to meet the needs of each respective group and address their particular concerns. Like effective bullfighters, superintendents know how and when to engage those in the audience to support their activities and projected positive outcomes.

Superintendents related to us that they worked comprehensively and intensively to address the various elements associated with ELCC Standard #4 in their respective communities. They often expressed that they focused on creating effective partnerships with all stakeholder groups and took time nurturing those groups and those relationships. This concept is well documented by researchers who cite the significance of partnership development for sustaining organizational changes.

Accordingly, Doolittle, Sudek, and Rattigan (2008) posit that "creating effective partnerships requires time upfront to establish ground rules, clarify the tasks to be undertaken, identify supports required for successful implementation, and ensure that a shared vision and mission exist between partners." They also contend that their research supports that "by focusing on a mutually agreed upon educational initiative and using a systematic change model, real work can be accomplished and even sustained" (2008).

Superintendents who effectively manage living on the horns of dilemmas insist that they know how to engage others in their projects, strategies, and activities so that others become leaders and continue the optimistic quest for positive outcomes. This leadership approach is consistent with the sage perspective of Lao-tzu (1954), who promoted an essential leadership style that he insisted incorporated, "Bearing yet not possessing, working yet not taking credit, leading yet not dominating . . . this is the primal virtue."

Michael Fullan (2006) also corroborates this perspective and further extends the impact of such an approach when he states that effective leaders, "can work within and keep developing cultures of purposeful collaboration" (71). Optimism becomes infectious and this is good for superintendents as well as bullfighters since it keeps others believing in and cheering for the performer.

The significance of optimism was frequently referred to by superintendents:

- "The job is overwhelming. Literally 24/7. But with a lot of effort and hours with frequent conversations with people that I respected . . . I now feel far more comfortable. I must admit it took a while but I have learned to live with a certain amount of tension." (Suburban school superintendent)
- "People who may disagree with you will give support if you are seen as a member of the community who cares about the welfare of the community. Love or hate you there is no question about the time you give to the community." (Rural school superintendent)
- "This is a privileged school district. Strong community support. He would do his best not to break it." (Suburban school superintendent)
- "Your head and heart as the district leader must always 'beat' an optimistic note!" (Rural school superintendent)
- "Whenever confronted with a troubling outcome—I make sure that that song from Annie ['Tomorrow'] keeps playing in my head—

because, YES—even in the dark nights of my superintendency—
tomorrow—the sun did come up—and another day with new issues began afresh—be positive in all you do!" (Suburban school
superintendent)

RESILIENCY—IRREPRESSIBLE SPIRIT FOR LEADING
TO MAKE A DIFFERENCE

Superintendents and matadors share the passion to be at the epicenter of
their respective arenas. They want to be in charge of the performance and
control the actions because they have an unbridled desire to lead and be
recognized for their inherent ability to make a difference in their respective arenas. They want to lead, they enjoy leading, and they look forward
to the challenges of leadership in such public arenas.

Successful superintendents, indeed, are driven from within to self-
actualize by significantly influencing the behaviors of others in the classical personal growth tradition espoused by Abraham Maslow (1968) in
Toward a Psychology of Being. Subsequently, they are not deterred by set-
backs or the occasional goring via the horns of their various metaphorical
and real bulls, but learn from each experience and further develop their
personal elasticity because they have the spirit to continue to lead.

Researchers have concluded that this resiliency disposition consists of
various key behaviors including "good decision-making skills, assertive-
ness, impulse control, and problem-solving skills as well as sense of hu-
mor, internal focus of control, autonomy, positive view of the future, self-
motivation, personal competence, and feelings of self-worth" (Henderson
and Milstein, 1996). Researchers currently contend that the above leadership resiliency disposition with its associated behaviors are both based on
personal nature and nurture but "resiliency or hardiness is a process
more than a list of traits and it can be learned" (Higgins, 1996).

Experience may be the "best teacher" for those desirous of improving
their resiliency quotient but the key ingredient is having belief in one's
self. Robert Fulghum (1992) presented to superintendents and other
school district leaders that the most effective leaders are resilient leaders
who learn from their experiences and develop new leadership strategies
to confront new dilemmas because of their passionate belief that if they
put their energy on the key "wheels of the organization," they can influence the "path of that vehicle." Consequently, resilient leaders passion-
ately want to and effectively do make a difference in education.

Superintendents and matadors possess an incredible resiliency factor
because of that passionate leadership spirit and most have developed a
calcified veneer that assists them in deflecting the horns of those ever-
charging bulls in their arenas. They constantly believe and act on their
most deeply held passionate beliefs that they, in fact, are the difference

makers in their arenas. Jim Collins (2001) has identified this type of thinking as having a "hedgehog" perspective in that it is a "simple frame of reference for their own behaviors" combined with a piercing insight into their own organizations and their mission.

Additional researchers have identified that resilient leaders possess the following key coping skills that further enhance their irrepressible spirit by:

- looking at life as a constant "challenge" and developing the ability to see change as an opportunity not a crisis (Csikszentmihalyi, 1990; Norton, 2005);
- exhibiting a strong "commitment" to themselves, their families, and their organizations (Kobasa et al., 1982; Kotter and Cohen, 2002);
- acting as if they can change their external world and not be changed by it (Cashman, 2008; Glasser, 1990; Quinn, 1996);
- possessing and demonstrating a deep creative urge and an inner compulsion to envision options in decision making (Blanchard and Waghorn, 1999; Collins, 2001; Csikszentmihalyi, 1990; Fullan, 2003);
- developing and sustaining personal relationships and employing their heart, mind, and soul to solve problems (Bolman and Deal, 1995; Cashman, 2008; DePree, 1989; Fullan, 2006).

The above coping skill factors that influence the development and refinement of an individual's resiliency quotient, (a) challenge; (b) commitment; (c) control; (d) creativity; and (e) caring have been specifically researched and articulated in a number of contemporary leadership literatures.

The general conclusion of these investigations is that effective school leaders employ those five key coping skills on a regular basis to further buttress their personal and professional resiliency so that they can effectively implement the concepts associated with the six ELCC Standards previously enumerated and continue their irrepressible leadership spirit to make a difference in education.

Practicing superintendents provided insights about resiliency:

- "As a new superintendent, my biggest mistake in initiating change was I thought hell, I am the superintendent . . . they should follow what I say! Big mistake!" (Small-city school superintendent)
- "When I was first hired as superintendent several of my colleagues from other nearby districts bought me a T-shirt that had the name of my school district on the front along with SUPERINTENDENT OF SCHOOLS in large letters—and on the back was a BIG BULL-SEYE! I think that was the most appropriate professional gift I ever received as during my over decade tenure in that superintendency, I used that T-shirt on a number of occasions to literally remind

everyone that I was willing to take the negative barbs and acerbic arrows for the district! My wearing of that T-shirt always resulted in reducing tensions and focusing everyone on my positive views of our mission." (Suburban school superintendent)

- "I often remind myself of that old saying, 'Power corrupts and absolute power corrupts absolutely'! So I try to 'curb my own' attraction to 'the power of the superintendency' which the previous superintendent in the district often used!" (Rural school superintendent)
- "Personally it hurt after solving several teacher issues, that the union issued a vote of no confidence. It took a while before I decided that it was important to identify problems where we had a mutual interest." (Small-city school superintendent)
- "Take your job seriously but never take yourself seriously. This is an important job but not your job. And be sure to take care of yourself." (Suburban school superintendent)
- "Every child has a right to receive a quality education." (Small-city school superintendent)

REFLECTION

1. Leaders as followers, followers as leaders, where does leadership and followership begin and end?
2. What key core processes, attributes, and skills do we need to put into our day-to-day practices to be effective school leaders?
3. What is your interpretation of "an effective school superintendent is only one important part of an effective school district but it may not be possible to have an effective school district without an effective school superintendent?"
4. What do school leaders need to know and do to enhance the process of "leadership for teaching and learning?"

Appendix

Framework for Original Research

The research for this book was conducted in 2010–2011, and is based upon the input of more than three hundred superintendents from various Mid-Atlantic states. The research design included four parts:

- Part A: Demographic Data
- Part B: Decision-making/Problem-solving Approaches
- Part C: Personal and Professional Dilemmas
- Part D: Opportunity to Reflect About Dilemmas

The survey (Part B) of the instrument included thirty-five statements gleaned from the research of Hoy and Tarter (2008), designed to gather information about the frequency of the following seven approaches used by educational leaders when confronting problems and making decisions associated with school administration: (1) Classical, (2) Incremental, (3) Garbage Can, (4) Shared Decision-Making, (5) Satisficing, (6) Mixed Scanning, and (7) Political. It was decided by the researchers that instead of the eight categories as initially enumerated by Hoy and Tarter, there would be seven approaches used for this survey.

The two categories associated with shared decision-making in the Hoy and Tarter (2008) text were combined into one to streamline the survey and make the survey user-friendly. The researchers and their associates had previously conducted a study that verified the significance of using this component of the survey instrument to measure decision-making and problem-solving approaches in school.

In addition, the list below provides a description of each of the seven decision-making categories used in this research based on the initial work of Hoy and Tarter (2008):

Seven Superintendent Decision-making Categories

1. Research category: Description of problem-solving approach.
2. Classical approach: Consists of a rational systematic means-ends analysis focused on optimizing organizational goals.
3. Incremental approach: Consists of a successive search for reasonable alternatives to facilitate good decision-making.
4. Garbage can approach: Involves scanning and using previously identified solutions to solve emerging problems.

5. Shared decision-making approach: Includes empowering others to assist in finding solutions to problems meaningful to them.
6. Satisficing approach: Involves making decisions that are acceptable to most of those impacted.
7. Mixed Scanning approach: Involves broad ends and tentative means that focus on adapting decisions to policy guidelines.
8. Political approach: Involves decisions that emerge spontaneously but are personally driven by the leader's need for power.

Of note is Part C, personal and professional dilemmas, which was designed to capture the frequency with which contemporary school superintendents confront various dilemmas associated with school leadership, decision-making, and problem solving. Twelve prominent dilemmas, developed from the leadership research during the past ninety years, were enumerated in the survey instrument and follow-up interviews. The dilemmas are:

- *Centralized vs. Decentralized Decision-Making*: Is it better for the superintendent to centralize and ultimately control the decision-making process rather than to decentralize and empower others to assume responsibility?
- *Personal Life vs. Professional Life*: Is the personal cost too high for the superintendent in terms of the dilemma with one's own family issues while trying to meet the time and stress demands of school leadership?
- *Truth vs. Varnished Truth*: Is it sometimes better and more humane for the superintendent to tell a half-truth than the whole truth to protect the interests and well-being of faculty and school site administrators, as well as the district as a whole?
- *Creativity vs. Discipline of Thought*: Is it possible to provide greater latitude of freedom for some school building leaders and still maintain structure for others who need such within a climate of collegiality?
- *Trust vs. Change*: Does implementing even the smallest organizational change result in suspicion of the superintendent's motives?
- *Leadership vs. Management*: How critical is it for the superintendents to understand the difference between leadership and management, and be able to put into practice one or the other when necessary?
- *Long-term Goals vs. Short-term Results*: How critical is it for superintendents' job security to focus on short-term improvements in areas such as student test scores rather than implementing comprehensive quality student-centered programs?
- *Motivation vs. Manipulation*: Is the superintendent authentically motivating teams to accomplish district goals rather than manipulating teams to get the results deemed most appropriate for your success and survival?

- *Independence vs. Dependence*: Does the superintendent readily and too often accept the role of the district problem solver and decision-maker rather than facilitate others to solve their own problems?
- *Conflict vs. Consensus*: Is it best for the superintendent to promote consensus in decision-making rather than to create dynamic tension that may result in conflict but more meaningful resolution to issues?
- *Commitment vs. Compliance*: Is it possible for the superintendent to achieve commitment during times of change that foster compliance given the bureaucratic nature and hierarchical chain of command found in contemporary education?
- *Problems vs. Predicaments*: Is the public able to understand that several critical contemporary educational problems are really systemic predicaments that are more universal in nature, and not easily solved at the local level?

References

Acton, Lord. (2001–2013). *Brainy Quote.* BookRags Media Network: www.brainquote.com/quotes/authors/y/yc.

Arnett, W. (1955). *Santayana and the Sense of Beauty.* Bloomington, Ind.: Indiana University Press.

Bandura, A. (1997). *Self-Efficacy: The Exercise of Control.* New York: W. H. Freeman.

Behrendt, S. (1992). *Reading William Blake.* London: Macmillan Press.

Bennis, W. (1989, 2009). *On Becoming a Leader.* Reading, Mass.: Addison-Wesley.

Bennis, W. and B. Nanus. (1985). *Leaders: The Strategies for Taking Charge.* New York: Harper & Row.

Berra, Yogi. (2001–2013). *Brainy Quote.* BookRags Media Network: www.brainquote.com/quotes/authors/y/yc.

Blanchard, K. and S. Johnson. (1986). *The One Minute Manager.* New York: William Morrow and Company.

Blanchard, K. and T. Waghorn. (1999). *Mission Impossible.* New York: McGraw-Hill.

Bolman, L. and T. Deal. (1991). *Reframing Organizations.* San Francisco: Jossey-Bass.

Bolman, L. and T. Deal. (1995, 2011). *Leading with Soul—An Uncommon of Spirit.* San Francisco: Jossey-Bass.

Brands, H. (1997). *T. R.: The Last Romantic.* New York: Basic Books.

Brown, H. B. (1972). *President N. Eldon Tanner: A Man of Integrity.* Salt Lake City, Utah: The Church of Jesus Christ of Latter Day Saints.

Brown, J. and C. Moffett. (1992). *The Hero's Journey: How Educators Can Transform Schools and Improve Learning.* Alexandria, Va.: ASCD.

Burns, G. (2001–2013). *Brainy Quote.* BookRags Media Network: www.brainquote.com/quotes/authors/y/yc.

Burns, J. M. (1978). *Leadership.* New York: Harper & Row.

Burns, J. M. (2003). *Transforming Leadership.* New York: Grove Press.

Calzi, F. (1974). *Analysis of the Current Status of Management by Objectives and the Development of a Management by Objectives Model For Use in School Districts.* Buffalo, N.Y.: State University of New York at Buffalo.

Calzi, F. (2010). "Berufliche und Personliche Dilemmata von Menschen in Schulleiterfunktionn" ("Critical Personal and Professional Dilemmas Facing School Leaders"—Translated into German). In P. Westermann and D. Berntzen (Hrsg.) *Kooperation in Schule und Unterrich: Implemenentationsansatze und perspekitiven.* Muenster, Deutschland: Zfl-Verlag, 129–136. http://dnb.ddb.de.

Camus, A. (1942). *The Myth of Sisyphus: And Other Essays.* Thousand Oaks, Calif.: Vintage Books.

Capra, F. (1946). *It's a Wonderful Life.* Hollywood, Calif.: Paramount Pictures.

Cashman, K. (2008). *Leadership from the Inside Out.* San Francisco: Berrett-Koehler Publishers, Inc.

Clark, D. (2006). *Descartes: A Biography.* Cambridge: Cambridge University Press.

Clemens, J. and M. Wolff. (1999). *Movies to Manage By.* New York: Contemporary Books.

Collins, J. (2001). *Good to Great—Why Some Companies Make The Leap . . . and Others Don't.* New York: HarperCollins.

Collins, J. and M. Hansen. (2011). *Great by Choice: Uncertainty, Chaos and Luck: Why Some Thrive Despite Them All.* New York: Harper Collins.

Conger, J. A. (1990). "The Dark Side of Leadership." *Organizational Dynamics* 19: 44–45.

Conner, D. (1993). *Managing at the Speed of Change*. New York: Villard.

Cooper, R. and A. Sawaf. (1997). *Executive e q: Emotional Intelligence in Leadership and Organizations*. New York: Berkley Press.

Cosier, R. and C. Schwenk. (1990). *Agreement and Thinking Alike: Ingredients for Poor Decisions*. Briarcliff Manor, N.Y.: Academy of Management.

Council of Chief State School Officers. (2008). Educational Leadership Policy Standards. Washington, DC: ISLLC.

Covey, S. (1989). *The 7 Habits of Highly Effective People*. New York: Fireside.

Covey, S. (1991). *Principle Centered Leadership*. New York: Fireside.

Creel, H. G. (1949). *Confucius: The Man and the Myth*. New York: John Day Company.

Csikszentmihalyi, M. (1990). *Flow: The Psychology of Optimal Experience*. New York: Harper & Row.

Deming, W. E. (1982). *Quality, Productivity and Competitive Position*. Cambridge, Mass.: MIT Center for Advanced Engineering.

Dentsen, I. L., and Gray, J. H. (2001). "Leadership Development and Reflection: What is the Connection?" *International Journal of Education* 3: 119–224. Bailrigg, U.K.: Lancaster University.

DePree, M. (1989). *Leadership Is an Art*. New York: Dell.

Dickens, C. (2012). *A Christmas Carol—The Original Manuscript*. Oxford, U.K.: Benediction Classics.

Doolittle, G., M. Sudek, and P. Rottigan. (2008). *Creating Professional Learning Communities: The Work of Professional Development Schools*. Columbus, Ohio: The Ohio State University.

Drucker, P. (1974). *Management*. New York: Harper & Row.

Drucker, P. (1989). *The New Realities*. New York: Harper & Row.

Drucker, P. (2006). *Innovation and Entrepreneurship*. New York: HarperCollins.

Duck, J. (2001). *Change Monster*. New York: Crown Press.

Duffy, F. (2006). *Power, Politics, and Ethics in School Districts*. Lanham, Md.: Rowman & Littlefield.

DuFour, R., and R. Eaker. (1998). *Professional Learning Communities at Work*. Alexandria, Va.: Solution Tree.

Duncan, P. (1995). *Mr. Holland's Opus*. Portland, OR: Buena Vista Pictures.

Durant W. (1954). *Lao Tzu: Our Oriental Heritage*. New York: Simon and Schuster.

Education Recovery Act. (2009). *Race to the Top*. Washington, D.C.: United Sates Department of Education.

Einstein, A. (2001–2013). *Brainy Quote*. BookRags Media Network: www.brainquote.com/quotes/authors/y/yc.

Erikson, E. (1970). *Gandhi's Truth*. New York: Norton.

Etzioni, A. (1964). *Modern Organizations*. New York: Prentice Hall.

Evans, R. (1996). *Christmas Every Day*. New York: Simon and Schuster.

Fayol, H. (1949). *General and Industrial Management*. London: Sir Isaac Pitman.

Feresten, S. (1995). *Seinfeld Season 7-Episode 6*.

Ferrell, R. (1994). *Harry S. Truman: A Life*. Columbia, Mo.: University of Missouri Press.

Franklin, B. (2001–2013). *Brainy Quote*. BookRags Media Network: www. brainquote.com/quotes/authors/y/yc.

Fulghum, R. (2003). *All I Need to Know I Learned in Kindergarten*. New York: Random House.

Fullan, M. (2001). *Leading in a Culture of Change*. San Francisco: Jossey-Bass.

Fullan, M. (2003). *The Moral Imperative of School Leadership*. Thousand Oaks, Calif.: Corwin Press.

Fullan, M. (2006). *Breakthrough*. Thousand Oaks, Calif.: Corwin Press.

Gandhi, M. (1999). *Vows and Observances*. Berkeley, Calif.: Berkeley Hills Books.

Gangi, Kelly, C. (2006). *Mother Teresa*. New York: Fall River Press.

Gardner, J. (1990). *On Leadership*. New York: The Free Press.

Glass, T. and L. Franceschini. (2007). *The State of the American Superintendency: A Mid-Decade Study*. Lanham, Md.: Rowman & Littlefield.

Glasser, W. (1990). *The Quality School: Managing Students Without Coercion*. New York: Harper Perennial.

Goals 2000. (1994). *Goals 2000: Educate America Act (P.L. 103-227)*. Washington, D.C.: U.S. Secretary of Education.

Goodrich, F. and A. Hackett. (1946). *Movie: It's A Wonderful Life*. Amazon.com Company.

Goodwin Kearns, D. (2005). *Team of Rivals*. New York: Simon & Schuster.

Goleman, D. (2002). *Primal Leadership*. Boston: Harvard Business School Press.

Greene, R. (1998). *The 48 Laws of Power*. New York: The Penguin Group.

Greenleaf, R. (1997). *Servant Leadership*. Mahwah, N.J.: Paulist Press.

Hall, G. and S. Hord. (2006). *Implementing Change: Patterns, Principles and Potholes*. Boston: Allyn and Bacon.

Hammond, J., R. L. Keeney, and H. Raiffa. (1998). *Smart Choices: A Practical Guide to Making Better Choices to Making Better Decisions*. Boston: Harvard Business Press.

Handy, C. (1994). *The Age of Paradox*. Boston: Harvard Business School Press.

Handy, C. (1995). *Gods of Management*. New York: Oxford University Press.

Handy, C. (1996). *Beyond Certainty*. Boston: Harvard Business School Press.

Harvey, J. (1988). *The Abilene Paradox and Other Meditations*. New York: Wiley and Sons.

Hemingway, E. (1949). *Hemingway*. New York: The Viking Press.

Henderson, N. and M. Milstein. (1996). *Resiliency in Schools: Making It Happen for Students and Educators*. Thousand Oaks, Calif.: Corwin Press.

Heller, J. (1961). *Catch-22*. New York: Simon and Schuster.

Hersey, P. and P. Blanchard. (1998). *Management of Organizational Behavior*. Englewood Cliffs, N.J.: Prentice Hall.

Higgins, E. T. (1996). *Social Psychology Handbook of Basic Principles*. New York: Guilford Press.

Hill, P., C. Campbell, and J. Harvey. (2000). *It Takes a City*. Washington, D.C.: Brookings Institution Press

Holmes, O. (1858). *The Autocrat at the Breakfast Table*. Boston: Atlantic Monthly.

Houston, P. and S. Sokolow. (2006). *The Spiritual Dimension of Leadership*. Thousand Oaks, Calif.: Corwin Press.

Hoy, W. and Miskel, C. (2008). *Educational Administration: Theory, Research, and Practice* (8th ed.). New York: McGraw-Hill.

Hoy, W. and Tarter, C. (2008). *Administrators Solving the Problems of Practice: Decision-Making Cases, Concepts and Consequences*. Boston: Allyn and Bacon.

Hughes, L. (2001). *Fight for Freedom and Other Writings on Civil Rights*. Columbia, Mo.: University of Missouri Press.

Hursh D. (2008). *High-Stakes Testing and the Decline of Teaching and Learning*. Lanham, Md.: Rowman & Littlefield.

ISLLC Standards. (2013). *National Policy Board for Educational Administrators*. Washington, D.C.: Council of Chief State School Officers.

Jehn, K. (1995). *The Dynamic Nature of Conflict: A Longitudinal Study of Intergroup Conflict and Group Performance*. In Press-Academy of Management Journal.

Jordan, D. S. (2001–2013). *Brainy Quote*. BookRags Media Network: www.brainquote.com/quotes/authors/y/yc.

Kanter, R. M. (1984). *The Change Masters: Innovation and Entrepreneurship in the American Corporation*. New York: Simon and Schuster.

King, M. L. (1967). *Where Do We Go From Here: Chaos or Community*. Boston: Beacon Press.

Klimek, K., E. Ritzenhein, and K. Sullivan. (2008). *Generative Leadership*. Thousand Oaks, Calif.: Corwin Press.

Kobasa S., Maddi, S., and Kahn, S. (1982). "Hardiness and Health: A Perspective Study." *Journal of Personality and Social Psychology*, 42(1), 168–177.

Kotter, J. and D. Cohen. (2002). *The Heart of Change*. Boston: Harvard Business School Press.

Kouzes, J. and B. Posner. (2007). *The Leadership Challenge*. San Francisco: Jossey-Bass.

Krass, P. (1998). *The Book of Leadership Wisdom*. New York: John Wiley.

Kreeft, P. (1963). *Between Heaven and Hell: A Dialog Somewhere Beyond Death with John L. Kennedy, C.S. Lewis and Aldous Huxley*. Downers Grove, Ill.: InterVarsity Press.

Lencioni, P. (2002). *The Five Dysfunctions of a Team—A Leadership Fable*. San Francisco: Jossey-Bass.

Lewin, K. (1947). *Frontiers in Group Dynamics*. Thousand Oaks, CA: Sage Publications.

Litchka, P., M. Fenzel, and W. Polka. (2009). "The Stress Process Among School Superintendents." *International Journal of Educational Leadership Preparation* 4(4). Retrieved from http://ijelp.expressacademic.org.

Lombardi, V. S. (2001–2013). *Brainy Quote*. BookRags Media Network: www. brainquote.com/quotes/authors/y/yc.

Loth, D. (1929). *Lorenzo the Magnificent*. New York: Cornwall Press.

Ludwig, E. (1932). *Goethe: The History of a Man*. New York: G. P. Putnam Sons.

Machiavelli, N. (1992). *The Prince (II Principe)*. New York: Dover Publications.

Marzano, R., T. Waters, and B. McNulty. (2005). *School Leadership That Works*. Washington, D.C.: Association for Supervision and Curriculum Development.

Maslow, Abraham. (1968). *Toward a Psychology of Being*. New York: John Wiley and Sons.

Maxwell, J. (2003). *Ethics 101*. New York: Center Street.

Marcu, V. S. (1939). *Accent on Power: The Life and Times of Machiavelli*. New York: Farrar & Rinehart.

Maslow, A. (1970). *Motivation and Personality*. New York: Harper & Row.

Maxwell, J. (1998). *The 21 Irrefutable Laws of Leadership*. Nashville, Tenn.: Thomas Nelson Publishers.

McGregor, D. (1966). *Leadership and Motivation*. Cambridge, Mass.: The MIT Press.

Mencken, H. L. (1949). *A Mencken Chrestomathy—His Own Selection of His Choicest Writings*. New York: Alfred A. Knopf.

Miller, L. M. (1984). *American Spirit: Visions of a New Corporate Culture*. New York: Morrow.

Miller, P. (2012). Self-Reflection: The Key to Effective Leadership. *Today's Manager*, December 2011–January 2012.

Morgan, G. (1997). *Images of Organization*. Thousand Oaks, Calif.: Sage Publications.

National Commission on Excellence in Education. (1983). *A Nation at Risk: The Imperative for Educational Reform*. Washington D.C.: Secretary of Education—United States Department of Education.

NCATE Standards. (2013). National Council for Accreditation of Teacher Education. Washington, D.C.

Niebuhr, R. (1932). *Moral Man and Immoral Society: A Study of Ethics and Politics*. New York: Charles Scribner's Sons.

Norton, M. S. (2005). *Competency Based Preparation of Educational Administrators: Tasks, Competencies and Indicators of Competency*. Tempe, Arizona: Arizona State University.

Nyberg, D. (1992). *The Varnished Truth: Truth Telling and Deceiving in Ordinary Life*. Chicago: The University of Chicago Press.

O'Brien, M. (1998). *Theodore M. Hesburgh: God Country and Notre Dame*. Notre Dame: University of Notre Dame Press.

O'Toole, J. (1996). *Leading Change—The Argument for Value Based Leadership*. New York: Ballantine Books.

Overton, J. (1993). *The Life of Robert Louis Stevenson for Boys and Girls*. New York: Charles Scribner's Sons.

Palmer, P. (2011). *Healing the Heart of Democracy—The Courage to Create a Politics Worthy of the Human Spirit*. San Francisco: Jossey Press.

Peters, T. and N. Austin. (1985). *A Passion for Excellence*. New York: Random House.

Peters, T. and R. Waterman. (1984). *In Search of Excellence*. New York: Harper & Row.

Picasso P. (2001–2013). *Brainy Quote.* BookRags Media Network: www.brainquote.com/quotes/authors/y/yc.

Plato. *Brainy Quote.* BookRags Media Network: www.brainquote.com/quotes/authors/y/yc.

Polka, W. and P. Litchka. (2008). *The Dark Side of Leadership: Superintendents and the Professional Victim Syndrome.* New York: Rowman & Littlefield.

Polka, W., P. Litchka, F. Calzi, S. Denig, and R. Mete. (2013). *Superintendent Decision-Making and Problem-Solving: Living on the Horns of Dilemmas.* NCPEA. Lancaster, Penn.: A Proactive Publications Book.

Quinn, R. (1996). *Deep Change: Discovering the Leader Within.* San Francisco: Jossey-Bass.

Rabey, J. (2014). *The Relationship between the Self-Efficacy of New York Superintendents of School and Their Self-Reflected Practices.* PhD Dissertation. Lewiston, NY: Niagara University.

Reavis, G. (1937). "Animal School." *Clearinghouse.* Retrieved October 6, 2009 from http://www.adrianwalsh.com.au/fable_of_the_animal_school.htm.

Roberts, Wes. (1985). *Leadership Secrets of Attila the Hun.* New York: Warner Books.

Roberts, Wes. (1995). *Make It So: Leadership Lessons From Star Trek: The Next Generation.* New York: Simon and Schuster.

Roscoe, G. (1994). *The Triple Gem: An Introduction to Buddhism.* Chiang Mai: Silkworm Books.

Rotberg, R. (1988). *The Founder: Cecil Rhodes and the Pursuit of Power.* Oxford: Oxford University Press.

Rubenstein, A. (1980). *My May Years.* New York: Alfred A. Knopf

Ruskin, J. and C. Tinker. (2012). *Selections from the Works of John Ruskin.* Charleston, SC: BiblioBazaar Reproduction Series.

Schlechty, P. (2001). *Shaking Up the School House.* San Francisco: Jossey-Bass.

Schopenhauer, A. (1974). *Parerga and Paralipomena: Short Philosophical Essays.* New York: Oxford University Press.

Senge, P. (1990). *The Fifth Discipline: The Art and Practice of the Learning Organization.* New York: Doubleday.

Sergiovanni, T. (1992). *Moral Leadership: Getting to the Heart of School Improvement.* San Francisco: Jossey-Bass.

Sharma, R. (1998). *Leadership Wisdom: From the Monk Who Sold His Ferrari.* Toronto: HarperCollins.

Shaw, G. B. (2001–2013). *Brainy Quote.* BookRags Media Network: www.brainquote.com/quotes/authors/y/yc.

Simons, T., and Peterson R. (2000). Task Conflict in Top Management Teams: Pivotal Role of Intergoup Trust. *Journal of Applied Psychology,* 85(1), 102–111.

Simon, H. (1997). *Administrative Behavior,* 4th Edition. New York: The Free Press.

Slavin, R. (1998). *Show Me The Evidence: Proven and Promising Programs for America's Schools.* London, Ontario: Sage Publications.

Snow, C. P. (1951). *The Masters.* New York: The Macmillan Company.

Stone, C. (2001). *Building Civic Capacity: The Politics of Reforming Urban Schools.* Lawrence, Kansas: University Press of Kansas.

Thoreau, H. (2001–2013). *Brainy Quote.* BookRags Media Network: www.brainquote.com/quotes/authors/y/yc.

Tichy, N. and W. Bennis. (2007). *Judgment: How Winning Leaders Make Great Calls.* New York: Penguin Group.

Twain, M. (2001–2013). *Brainy Quote.* BookRags Media Network: www.brainquote.com/quotes/authors/y/yc.

Vroom V. S. and P. Yetton. (1973). *Leadership and Decision-Making.* Pittsburgh: University of Pittsburgh Press.

Wallace Foundation. (2013). *Six Districts Begin the Principal Pipeline Initiative.* New York: Wallace Foundation.

Made in the USA
Middletown, DE
06 January 2025

68944464R00083